GEORGE ORWELL

Modern Critical Views

These and other titles in preparation

Modern Critical Views

GEORGE ORWELL

Edited and with an introduction by
Harold Bloom
Sterling Professor of the Humanities
Yale University

CHELSEA HOUSE PUBLISHERS ◇ 1987
New York ◇ New Haven ◇ Philadelphia

© 1986 by Chelsea House Publishers, a division of Chelsea
House Educational Communications, Inc.
   95 Madison Avenue, New York, NY 10016
   345 Whitney Avenue, New Haven, CT 06511
   5014 West Chester Pike, Edgemont, PA 19028

Introduction © 1987 by Harold Bloom

Printed and bound in the United States of America

∞The paper used in this publication meets the minimum
requirements of the American National Standard for
Permanence of Paper for Printed Library Materials,
Z39.48-1984.

Library of Congress Cataloging-in-Publication Data
George Orwell.
   (Modern critical views)
   Bibliography: p.
   Includes index.
   1. Orwell, George, 1903–1950—Criticism and
interpretation.
I. Bloom, Harold.   II. Series.
PR6029.R8Z638   1987   828'.91209   86-17610
ISBN 0-87754-648-7

Contents

Editor's Note

This volume gathers together a representative selection of the best criticism yet published on the writings of George Orwell, arranged in the chronological order of its original publication. I am grateful to Peter Childers for his insight and erudition in helping me to edit this book.

My introduction questions the aesthetic achievement of *1984*, while acknowledging the narrative's considerable moral force. Such a force can be exerted by a period piece, such as *Uncle Tom's Cabin*, and it seems just to speculate that *1984* may become a period piece in its turn.

The chronological sequence begins with the most distinguished of living literary scholars, the Canadian critic Northrop Frye, who reviews *Animal Farm* and finds it wanting as an allegory of motivation. Philip Rahv, analyzing *1984*, denies its aesthetic validity, yet grants it the status and function of a perpetually timely warning.

In a revaluation of *Burmese Days*, Malcolm Muggeridge finds it to be a readable period piece that reflects the literary influence of Kipling. Sir Herbert Read, though aware of the difficulties of such a comparison, analogizes Orwell to Defoe, finding in *1984* the *Robinson Crusoe* of our time.

In the most formidable essay yet ventured on Orwell, Lionel Trilling introduces *Homage to Catalonia* as the portrait of an authentic truthseeker, whose devotion to the workers of Barcelona survived the betrayal of the anarchists by their supposed allies the Communists. The eminent sociologist and Freud scholar Philip Rieff, discussing *A Clergyman's Daughter,* analyzes Orwell's position both as the saint of liberals and as the critic of the post-liberal imagination, embodied for Orwell in Henry Miller.

Richard Wollheim, distinguished philosopher and another outstanding Freudian, reconsiders *The Road to Wigan Pier* and judges its flaws to be those of its age, when journalism and literature could not be distinguished. In a reading of *Keep the Aspidistra Flying*, Nicholas Guild concentrates upon the curious effect of the novel's conclusion, where the hero yields to societal reality, clearly with Orwell's approval, although critics generally see this ending as a great defeat. *Coming Up for Air* is judged to be Orwell's apocalypse or central visionary work by Jeffrey Meyers, whose comparison of Orwell and Henry Miller contrasts interestingly with Rieff's essay.

In a subtle study of how Orwell's ambivalences qualify his overt ironies, Cleo McNelly Kearns suggests that our current idolatry of Orwell as an exemplary prose stylist and moral essayist may have touched its outer limits. Orwell is again judged to be naïve, this time as a theorist of language, in a pungent dismissal by Roy Harris. George Woodcock rises to Orwell's defense by emphasizing that he was essentially a working journalist, rather than a novelist, and so remains fresh and valid through his awareness of the ways in which language has been betrayed by our age. Finally, Vita Fortunati examines *1984* against the literary tradition of utopias and provides us with a dialectical reading of the narrative.

Introduction

There is an equivocal irony to reading, and writing, about George Orwell in 1986. I have just reread *1984, Animal Farm,* and many of the essays for the first time in some years, and I find myself lost in an interplay of many contending reactions, moral and aesthetic. Orwell, aesthetically considered, is a far better essayist than a novelist. Lionel Trilling, reviewing *1984,* in 1984, praised the book, with a singular moral authority:

> The whole effort of the culture of the last hundred years has been directed toward teaching us to understand the economic motive as the irrational road to death, and to seek salvation in the rational and the planned. Orwell marks a turn in thought; he asks us to consider whether the triumph of certain forces of the mind, in their naked pride and excess, may not produce a state of things far worse than any we have ever known. He is not the first to raise the question, but he is the first to raise it on truly liberal or radical grounds, with no intention of abating the demand for a just society, and with an overwhelming intensity and passion. This priority makes his book a momentous one.

The book remains momentous; perhaps it always will be so. But there is nothing intrinsic to the book that will determine its future importance. Its very genre will be established by political, social, economic events. Is it satire or science fiction or dystopia or countermanifesto? Last week I read newspaper accounts of two recent speeches, perorations delivered by President Reagan and by Norman Podhoretz, each favorably citing Orwell. The President, awarding medals to Senator Barry Goldwater and Helen Hayes, among others, saw them as exemplars of Orwell's belief in freedom and individual dignity, while the sage Podhoretz allowed himself to observe that Orwell would have become a neoconservative had he but survived until this moment. Perhaps irony, however equivocal, is inadequate to represent so curious a posthumous fate as has come to the author of *Homage to Catalonia,* a man who went to Barcelona to fight for the Party of Marxist Unity and the Anarcho-Syndicalists.

V. S. Pritchett and others were correct in describing Orwell as the best of modern pamphleteers. A pamphlet certainly can achieve aesthetic eminence; "tracts and pamphlets" is a major genre, particularly in Great Britain, where its masters include Milton, Defoe, Swift, Dr. Johnson, Burke, Blake, Shelley, Carlyle, Ruskin, and Newman. Despite his celebrated mastery of the plain style, it is rather uncertain that Orwell has joined himself to that company. I suspect that he is closer to the category that he once described as "good bad books," giving Harriet Beecher Stowe's *Uncle Tom's Cabin* as a supreme instance. Aesthetically considered, *1984* is very much the *Uncle Tom's Cabin* of our time, with poor Winston Smith as Uncle Tom, the unhappy Julia as little Eva, and the more-than-sadistic O'Brien as Simon Legree. I do not find O'Brien to be as memorable as Simon Legree, but then that is part of Orwell's point. We have moved into a world in which our torturers also have suffered a significant loss of personality.

II

Orwell's success as a prophet is necessarily a mixed one, since his relative crudity as a creator of character obliges us to read *1984* rather literally. What works best in the novel is its contextualization of all the phrases it has bequeathed to our contemporary language, though whether to *the* language is not yet certain. Newspeak and doublethink, "War Is Peace," "Freedom Is Slavery," "Ignorance Is Strength," "Big Brother Is Watching You," the Thought Police, the Two Minutes Hate, the Ministry of Truth, and all the other Orwellian inventions that are now wearisome clichés, are restored to some force, though little freshness, when we encounter them where they first arose.

Unfortunately, in itself that does not suffice. Even a prophetic pamphlet requires eloquence if we are to return to it and find ourselves affected at least as much as we were before. *1984* can hurt you a single time, and most likely when you are young. After that, defensive laughter becomes the aesthetic problem. Rereading *1984* can be too much like watching a really persuasive horror movie; humor acquires the validity of health. Contemporary reviewers, even Trilling, were too overwhelmed by the book's relevance to apprehend its plain badness as narrative or Orwell's total inability to represent even a curtailed human personality or moral character. Mark Schorer's response in the *New York Times Book Review* may have seemed appropriate on June 12, 1949, but its hyperboles now provoke polite puzzlement:

> No real reader can neglect this experience with impunity. He will be moved by Smith's wistful attempts to remember a different kind of life from his. He will make a whole new discovery of the beauty of love between man and woman, and of the strange beauty of landscape in a totally mechanized world. He will be asked to read through pages of sustained physical and psychological pain that have seldom been equaled and never in such quiet, sober prose. And he will return to his own life from Smith's escape into living death with a resolution to resist power wherever it means to deny him his individuality, and to resist for himself the poisonous lures of power.

Would it make a difference now if Orwell had given his book the title: "1994"? Our edge of foreboding has vanished when we contemplate the book, if indeed we ought to regard it as a failed apocalypse. Yet all apocalypses, in the literary sense, are failed apocalypses, so that if they fade, the phenomenon of literary survival or demise clearly takes precedence over whatever status social prophecy affords. The limits of Orwell's achievement are clarified if we juxtapose it directly to the authentic American apocalypses of our time: Faulkner's *As I Lay Dying*, Nathanael West's *Miss Lonelyhearts*, Thomas Pynchon's *Gravity's Rainbow*. Why do they go on wounding us, reading after reading, while *1984* threatens to become a period piece, however nightmarish? It would be absurdly unfair to look at *1984* side by side with Kafka and Beckett; Orwell was in no way an aspirant after the sublime, however demonic or diminished. But he was a satirist, and in *1984* a kind of phantasmagoric realist. If his O'Brien is not of the stature of the unamiable Simon Legree, he is altogether nonexistent as a Satanic rhetorician if we attempt to bring him into the company of West's Shrike.

Can a novel survive praise that endlessly centers upon its author's humane disposition, his indubitable idealism, his personal honesty, his political courage, his moral nature? Orwell may well have been the exemplary and representative Socialist intellectual of our time (though Raymond Williams, the crucial Marxist literary critic in Great Britain, definitely does not think so). But very bad men and women have written superb novels, and great moralists have written unreadable ones. *1984* is neither superb nor unreadable. If it resembles the work of a precursor figure, that figure is surely H. G. Wells, as Wyndham Lewis shrewdly realized. Wells surpasses Orwell in storytelling vigor, in pungency of characterization, and in imaginative invention, yet Wells now seems remote and Orwell remains very close. We are driven back to what makes *1984* a good bad book: relevance. The book substitutes for a real and universal fear: that in the political and economic area, the dreadful is still about to happen. Yet the book again lacks a defense against its own blunderings into the ridiculous. As social prophecy, it is closer to Sinclair Lewis's now forgotten *It Can't Happen Here* than to Nathanael West's still hilarious *A Cool Million,* where Big Brother, under the name of Shagpoke Whipple, speaks uncannily in the accents shared by Calvin Coolidge and Ronald Reagan. Why could not Orwell have rescued his book by some last touch of irony or by a valid invocation of the satiric Muse?

III

What Max Horkheimer and T. W. Adorno grimly called the Culture Industry has absorbed Orwell, and his *1984* in particular. Is this because Orwell retains such sentimentalities or soft idealisms as the poignance of true love? After all, Winston and Julia are terrorized out of love by brute pain and unendurable fear; no one could regard them as having been culpable in their forced abandonment of one another. This is akin to Orwell's fantastic and wholly unconvincing hope that the proles might yet offer salvation, a hope presumably founded upon the odd notion that Oceania lets eighty-five percent of its population go back to nature in the slums of London and other cities. Love and the working class are therefore pretty much undamaged in Orwell's vision. Contrast Pynchon's imaginative "paranoia" in *Gravity's Rainbow,* where all of us, of whatever social class, live in the Zone which is dominated by the truly paranoid System, and where authentic love can be represented only as sado-masochism. There is a Counterforce in *Gravity's Rainbow* that fights the System, but it is ineffectual, farcical, and can be animated only by the peculiar ideology that Pynchon calls sado-anarchism, an ideology that the Culture Industry cannot absorb, and that I suspect Adorno gladly would have embraced.

I don't intend this introduction as a drubbing or trashing of Orwell and *1984*, and *Gravity's Rainbow,* being an encyclopedic prose epic, is hardly a fair agonist against which *1984* should be matched. But the aesthetic badness of *1984* is palpable enough, and I am a good enough disciple of the divine Oscar Wilde to wonder if an aesthetic inadequacy really can be a moral splendor? Simon Legree beats poor old Uncle Tom to death, and O'Brien pretty well wrecks Winston Smith's body and then reduces him to supposed ruin by threatening him with some particularly nasty and hungry rats. Is *Uncle Tom's Cabin* actually a moral achievement, even if Harriet Beecher Stowe hastened both the Civil War and the Emancipation Proclamation? Is *1984* a moral triumph, even if it hastens a multiplication of neoconservatives?

The defense of a literary period piece cannot differ much from a defense of period pieces in clothes, household objects, popular music, movies, and the lower reaches of the visual arts. A period piece that is a political and social polemic, like *Uncle Tom's Cabin* and *1984,* acquires a curious charm of its own. What partly saves *1984* from Orwell's overliteralness and failures in irony is the strange archaism of its psychology and rhetoric:

> He paused for a few moments, as though to allow what he had been saying to sink in.
> "Do you remember," he went on, "writing in your diary, 'Freedom is the freedom to say that two plus two make four'?"
> "Yes," said Winston.
> O'Brien held up his left hand, its back toward Winston, with the thumb hidden and the four fingers extended.
> "How many fingers am I holding up, Winston?"
> "Four."
> "And if the Party says that it is not four but five—then how many?"
> "Four."
> The word ended in a gasp of pain. The needle of the dial had shot up to fifty-five. The sweat had sprung out all over Winston's body. The air tore into his lungs and issued again in deep groans which even by clenching his teeth he could not stop. O'Brien watched him, the four fingers still extended. He drew back the lever. This time the pain was only slightly eased.
> "How many fingers, Winston?"
> "Four."
> The needle went up to sixty.
> "How many fingers, Winston?"
> "Four! Four! What else can I say? Four!"

The needle must have risen again, but he did not look at it. The heavy, stern face and the four fingers filled his vision. The fingers stood up before his eyes like pillars, enormous, blurry, and seeming to vibrate, but unmistakably four.

"How many fingers, Winston?"

"Four! Stop it, stop it! How can you go on? Four! Four!"

"How many fingers, Winston?"

"Five! Five! Five!"

"No, Winston, that is no use. You are lying. You still think there are four. How many fingers, please?"

"Four! Five! Four! Anything you like. Only stop it, stop the pain!"

Abruptly he was sitting up with O'Brien's arm round his shoulders. He had perhaps lost consciousness for a few seconds. The bonds that had held his body down were loosened. He felt very cold, he was shaking uncontrollably. His teeth were chattering, the tears were rolling down his cheeks. For a moment he clung to O'Brien like a baby, curiously comforted by the heavy arm round his shoulders. He had the feeling that O'Brien was his protector, that the pain was something that came from outside, from some other source, and that it was O'Brien who would save him from it.

"You are a slow learner, Winston," said O'Brien gently.

"How can I help it?" he blubbered. "How can I help seeing what is in front of my eyes? Two and two are four."

"Sometimes. Winston. Sometimes they are five. Sometimes they are three. Sometimes they are all of them at once. You must try harder. It is not easy to become sane."

He laid Winston down on the bed. The grip on his limbs tightened again, but the pain had ebbed away and the trembling had stopped, leaving him merely weak and cold. O'Brien motioned with his head to the man in the white coat, who had stood immobile throughout the proceedings. The man in the white coat bent down and looked closely into Winston's eyes, felt his pulse, laid an ear against his chest, tapped here and there; then he nodded to O'Brien.

"Again," said O'Brien.

The pain flowed into Winston's body. The needle must be at seventy, seventy-five. He had shut his eyes this time. He knew that the fingers were still there, and still four. All that mattered was somehow to stay alive until the spasm was over. He had ceased to notice whether he was crying out or not. The pain lessened again. He opened his eyes. O'Brien had drawn back the lever.

"How many fingers, Winston?"

"Four. I suppose there are four. I would see five if I could. I am trying to see five."

"Which do you wish: to persuade me that you see five, or really to see them?"

"Really to see them."

"Again," said O'Brien.

If we took this with high seriousness, then its offense against any persuasive mode of representation would make us uneasy. But it *is* a grand period piece, parodying not only Stalin's famous trials, but many theologically inspired ordeals before the advent of the belated Christian heresy that Russian Marxism actually constitutes. Orwell was a passionate moralist, and an accomplished essayist. The age drove him to the composition of political romance, though he lacked nearly all of the gifts necessary for the writer of narrative fiction. *1984* is an honorable aesthetic failure, and perhaps time will render its crudities into so many odd period graces, remnants of a vanished era. Yet the imagination, as Wallace Stevens once wrote, is always at the end of an era. Lionel Trilling thought that O'Brien's torture of Winston Smith was "a hideous parody on psychotherapy and the Platonic dialogues." Thirty-seven years after Trilling's review, the scene I have quoted above seems more like self-parody, as though Orwell's narrative desperately sought its own reduction, its own outrageous descent into the fallacy of believing that only the worst truth about us can be the truth.

Orwell was a dying man as he wrote the book, suffering the wasting away of his body in consumption. D. H. Lawrence, dying the same way, remained a heroic vitalist, as his last poems and stories demonstrate. But Lawrence belonged to literary culture, to the old, high line of transcendental seers. What wanes and dies in *1984* is not the best of George Orwell, not the pamphleteer of *The Lion and the Unicorn* nor the autobiographer of *Homage to Catalonia* nor the essayist of *Shooting an Elephant*. That Orwell lived and died an independent Socialist, hardly Marxist but really a Spanish Anarchist, or an English dissenter and rebel of the line of Cromwell and of Cromwell's celebrators, Milton and Carlyle. *1984* has the singular power, not aesthetic but social, of being the product of an age, and not just of the man who set it down.

NORTHROP FRYE

Orwell and Marxism

George Orwell's satire on Russian Communism, *Animal Farm*, has just appeared in America, but its fame has preceded it, and surely by now everyone has heard of the fable of the animals who revolted and set up a republic on the farm, how the pigs seized control and how, led by a dictatorial boar named Napoleon, they finally became human beings walking on two legs and carrying whips, just as the old Farmer Jones had done. At each stage of this receding revolution, one of the seven principles of the original rebellion becomes corrupted, so that "no animal shall kill any other animal" has added to it the words "without cause" when there is a great slaughter of the so-called sympathizers of an exiled pig named Snowball, and "no animal shall sleep in a bed" takes on "with sheets" when the pigs move into the human farmhouse and monopolize its luxuries. Eventually there is only one principle left, modified to "all animals are equal, but some are more equal than others," as Animal Farm, its name changed back to Manor Farm, is welcomed into the community of human farms again after its neighbors have realized that it makes its "lower" animals work harder on less food than any other farm, so that the model workers' republic becomes a model of exploited labor.

The story is very well written, especially the Snowball episode, which suggests that the Communist "Trotskyite" is a conception on much the same mental plane as the Nazi "Jew," and the vicious irony of the end of Boxer the workhorse is perhaps really great satire. On the other hand, the

---

From *Northrop Frye: On Culture and Literature: A Collection of Review Essays*, edited by Robert D. Denham, © 1978 by the University of Chicago. University of Chicago Press, 1978. This essay originally appeared in *The Canadian Forum* 26 (December 1946).

satire on the episode corresponding to the German invasion seems to me
both silly and heartless, and the final metamorphosis of pigs into humans
is a fantastic disruption of the sober logic of the tale. The reason for the
change in method was to conclude the story by showing the end of Communism under Stalin as a replica of its beginning under the Czar. Such an
alignment is, of course, completely nonsense, and as Mr. Orwell must
know it to be nonsense, his motive for adopting it was presumably that he
did not know how otherwise to get his allegory rounded off with a neat,
epigrammatic finish.

Animal Farm adopts one of the classical formulas of satire, the corruption of principle by expediency, of which Swift's Tale of a Tub is the
greatest example. It is an account of the bogging down of Utopian aspira-
tions in the quicksand of human nature which could have been written by
a contemporary of Artemus Ward about one of the cooperative communi-
ties attempted in America during the last century. But for the same reason,
it completely misses the point as satire on the Russian development of
Marxism, and as expressing the disillusionment which many men of good-
will feel about Russia. The reason for that disillusionment would be much
better expressed as the corruption of expediency by principle. For the
whole point about Marxism was surely that it was the first revolutionary
movement in history which attempted to start with a concrete historical
situation instead of vast, a priori generalizations of the "all men are equal"
type, and which aimed at scientific rather than Utopian objectives. Marx
and Engels worked out a revolutionary technique based on an analysis of
history known as dialectical materialism, which appeared in the nineteenth
century at a time when metaphysical materialism was a fashionable creed,
but which Marx and Engels always insisted was a quite different thing
from metaphysical materialism.

Today, in the Western democracies, the Marxist approach to historical and economic problems is, whether he realizes it or not, an inseparable
part of the modern educated man's consciousness, no less than electrons
or dinosaurs, while metaphysical materialism is as dead as the dodo, or
would be if it were not for one thing. For a number of reasons, chief
among them the comprehensiveness of the demands made on a revolutionary by a revolutionary philosophy, the distinction just made failed utterly
to establish itself in practice as it did in theory. Official Marxism today
announces on page one that dialectical materialism is to be carefully distinguished from metaphysical materialism, and then insists from page two to
the end that Marxism is nevertheless a complete materialist metaphysic of
experience, with materialist answers to such questions as the existence of

God, the origin of knowledge, and the meaning of culture. Thus, instead of including itself in the body of modern thought and giving a revolutionary dynamic to that body, Marxism has become a self-contained dogmatic system, and one so exclusive in its approach to the remainder of modern thought as to appear increasingly antiquated and sectarian. Yet this metaphysical materialism has no other basis than that of its original dialectic, its program of revolutionary action. The result is an absolutizing of expediency which makes expediency a principle in itself. From this springs the reckless intellectual dishonesty which it is so hard not to find in modern Communism, and which is naturally capable of rationalizing any form of action, however ruthless.

A really searching satire on Russian Communism, then, would be more deeply concerned with the underlying reasons for its transformation from a proletarian dictatorship into a kind of parody of the Catholic church. Mr. Orwell does not bother with motivation: he makes his Napoleon inscrutably ambitious and lets it go at that, and, as far as he is concerned, some old reactionary bromide like "you can't change human nature" is as good a moral as any other for his fable. But he, like Koestler, is an example of a large number of writers in the Western democracies who during the last fifteen years have done their level best to adopt the Russian interpretation of Marxism as their own world outlook and have failed. The last fifteen years have witnessed a startling decline in the prestige of Communist ideology in the arts, and some of the contemporary changes in taste which have resulted will be examined in future contributions to this column.

PHILIP   RAHV

The Unfuture of Utopia

George Orwell has been able to maintain an exceptional position among the writers of our time seriously concerned with political problems. His work has grown in importance and relevance through the years, evincing a steadiness of purpose and uncommon qualities of character and integrity that set it quite apart from the typical products of the radical consciousness in this period of rout and retreat. A genuine humanist in his commitments, a friend, that is, not merely of mankind but of man (man as he is, not denatured by ideological abstractions), Orwell has gone through the school of the revolutionary movement without taking over its snappishly doctrinaire attitudes. His attachment to the primary traditions of the British empirical mind has apparently rendered him immune to dogmatism. Nor has the release from certitude lately experienced by the more alert radical intellectuals left him in the disoriented state in which many of his contemporaries now find themselves. Above all endowed with a strong sense of reality, he has neither played the prophet in or out of season nor indulged in that willful and irresponsible theorizing at present so much in vogue in certain radical quarters where it is mistaken for independent thought. It can be said of Orwell that he is the best kind of witness, the most reliable and scrupulous. All the more appalling, then, is the vision not of the remote but of the very close future evoked in his new novel, *1984*—a vision entirely composed of images of loss, disaster, and unspeakable degradation.

From *Literature and the Sixth Sense.* © 1969 by Philip Rahv. Houghton Mifflin, 1969. This essay originally appeared in *Partisan Review* 16, no. 7 (1949).

This is far and away the best of Orwell's books. As a narrative it has tension and actuality to a terrifying degree; still it will not do to judge it primarily as a literary work of art. Like all utopian literature, from Sir Thomas More and Campanella to William Morris, Bellamy, and Huxley, its inspiration is scarcely such as to be aesthetically productive of ultimate or positive significance; this seems to be true of utopian writings regardless of the viewpoint from which the author approaches his theme. *1984* chiefly appeals to us as a work of the political imagination, and the appeal is exercised with gravity and power. It documents the crisis of socialism with greater finality than Koestler's *Darkness at Noon,* to which it will be inevitably compared, since it belongs, on one side of it, to the same genre, the melancholy mid-century genre of lost illusions and Utopia betrayed.

While in Koestler's novel there are still lingering traces of nostalgia for the Soviet Utopia, at least in its early heroic phase, and fleeting tenderness for its protagonists, betrayers and betrayed—some are depicted as Promethean types wholly possessed by the revolutionary dogma and annihilated by the consequences of their own excess, the *hubris* of Bolshevism—in Orwell's narrative the further stage of terror that has been reached no longer permits even the slightest sympathy for the revolutionaries turned totalitarian. Here Utopia is presented, with the fearful simplicity of a trauma, as the abyss into which the future falls. The traditional notion of Utopia as the future good is thus turned inside out, inverted—nullified. It is now sheer mockery to speak of its future. Far more accurate it is to speak of its *unfuture.* (The addition of the negative affix "un" is a favorite usage of Newspeak, the official language of Ingsoc—English socialism—a language in which persons purged by the Ministry of Love, i.e., the secret police, are invariably described as *unpersons.* The principles of Newspeak are masterfully analyzed by Orwell in the appendix to his book. Newspeak is nothing less than a plot against human consciousness, for its sole aim is so to reduce the range of thought through the destruction of words as to make "*thoughtcrime* literally impossible because there will be no words in which to express it.")

The prospect of the future drawn in this novel can on no account be taken as a fantasy. If it inspires dread above all, that is precisely because its materials are taken from the real world as we know it, from conditions now prevailing in the totalitarian nations, in particular the Stalinist nations, and potentially among us too. Ingsoc, the system established in Oceania, the totalitarian super-State that unites the English-speaking peoples, is substantially little more than an extension into the near future of the present structure and policy of Stalinism, an extension as ingenious as it is logical, predicated upon conditions of permanent war and the development of the technical means of espionage and surveillance to the point of the complex extinction of private life. Big Brother, the supreme dictator of Oceania, is obviously modeled on Stalin, both in his physical features and in his literary style ("a style at once military and pedantic, and, because of a trick of asking questions and then promptly answering them . . . easy to imitate"). And who is Goldstein, the dissident leader of Ingsoc against whom Two Minute Hate Periods are conducted in all Party offices, if not Trotsky, the grand heresiarch and useful scapegoat, who is even now as indispensable to Stalin as Goldstein is shown to be to Big Brother? The inserted chapters from Goldstein's imaginary book on "The Theory and Practice of Oligarchical Collectivism," are a wonderfully realized imitation not only of Trotsky's characteristic rhetoric but also of his mode and manner as a Marxist theoretician. Moreover, the established pieties of Communism are at once recognizable in the approved spiritual regimen of the Ingsoc Party faithful: "A Party member is expected to have no private emotions and no respites from enthusiasm. He is supposed to live in a continuous frenzy of hatred of foreign enemies and internal traitors, triumph over victories, and self-abasement before the power and wisdom of the Party." One of Orwell's best strokes in his analysis of the technique of "doublethink," drilled into the Party members, which consists of the willingness to assert that black is white when the Party demands it, and even to believe that black is white, while at the same time knowing very well that nothing of the sort can be true. Now what is "doublethink," actually, if not the technique continually practiced by the Communists and their liberal collaborators, dupes, and apologists. Nor is it a technique available exclusively to Soviet citizens. Right here in New York any issue of *The Daily Worker* or of *The Daily Compass* will provide you with illustrations of it as vicious and ludicrous as any you will come upon in Orwell's story. As for "the control of the past," of which so much is made in Oceania through the revision of all records and the manipulation of memory through force and fraud, that too is by no means unknown in Russia, where periodically not only political history but also the history of art and literature are revamped in accordance with the latest edicts of the regime. The one feature of Oceanic society that appears to be really new is the proscription of sexual pleasure. The fact is, however, that a tendency in that direction has long been evident in Russia, where a new kind of prudery, disgusting in its unctuousness and hypocrisy, is officially promoted. In Oceania "the only recognized purpose of marriage was to beget children for the service of the Party." The new Russian laws regulating sexual relations are manifestly designed with the same purpose in mind. It is plain that any society which imposes a ban on personal experience must sooner or later distort and inhibit the sexual instinct. The totalitarian State cannot tolerate attachments between men and women that fall outside the political sphere and that are in their very nature difficult to control from above.

The diagnosis of the totalitarian perversion of socialism that Orwell makes in this book is far more remarkable than the prognosis it contains. This is not to deny that the book is prophetic; but its importance is mainly in its powerful engagement with the present. Through the invention of a society of which he can be imaginatively in full command, Orwell is enabled all the more effectively to probe the consequences for the human soul of the system of oligarchic collectivism—the system already prevailing in a good part of the world, which millions of people even this side of the Iron Curtain believe to be true-blue socialism and which at this time constitutes a formidable threat to free institutions. Hence to read this novel simply as a flat prediction of what is to come is to misread it. It is not a writ of fatalism to bind our wills. Orwell makes no attempt to persuade us, for instance, that the English-speaking nations will inevitably lose their freedom in spite of their vigorous democratic temper and libertarian traditions. "Wave of the future" notions are alien to Orwell. His intention, rather, is to prod the Western world into a more conscious and militant resistance to the totalitarian virus to which it is now exposed.

As in *Darkness at Noon,* so in *1984* one of the major themes is the psychology of capitulation. Winston Smith, the hero of the novel, is shown arming himself with ideas against the Party and defying it by forming a sexual relationship with Julia; but from the first we know that he will not escape the secret police, and after he is caught we see him undergoing a dreadful metamorphosis which burns out his human essence, leaving him a wreck who can go on living only by becoming one of "them." The closing sentences of the story are the most pitiful of all: "He had won a victory over himself. He loved Big Brother." The meaning of the horror of the last section of the novel, with its unbearable description of the torture of Smith by O'Brien, the Ingsoc Commissar, lies in its disclosure of a truth that the West still refuses to absorb. Hence the widespread mystifications produced by the Moscow Trials ("Why did they confess?") and, more recently, by the equally spectacular displays of confessional ardor in Russia's satellite states (Cardinal Mindszenty and others). The truth is that the modern totalitarians have devised a methodology of terror that enables them to break human beings by getting inside them. They explode the human character from within, exhibiting the pieces as the irrefutable proof of their own might and virtue. Thus Winston Smith begins with the notion that even if nothing else in the world was his own, still there were a few cubic centimeters inside his skull that belonged to him alone. But O'Brien, with his torture instruments and ruthless dialectic of power, soon teaches him that even these few cubic centimeters can never belong to him, only to the Party. What is so implacable about the despotisms of the twentieth century is that they have abolished martyrdom. If all through history the capacity and willingness to suffer for one's convictions served at once as the test and demonstration of sincerity, valor, and heroic resistance to evil, now even that capacity and willingness have been rendered meaningless. In the prisons of the M.V.D. or the Ministry of Love suffering has been converted into its opposite—into the ineluctable means of surrender. The victim crawls before his torturer, he identifies himself with him and grows to love him. That is the ultimate horror.

The dialectic of power is embodied in the figure of O'Brien, who simultaneously recalls and refutes the ideas of Dostoyevski's Grand Inquisitor. For a long time we thought that the legend of the Grand Inquisitor contained the innermost secrets of the power-mongering human mind. But no, modern experience has taught us that the last word is by no means to be found in Dostoyevski. For even the author of *The Brothers Karamazov,* who wrote that "man is a despot by nature and loves to be a torturer," was for all his crucial insights into evil nevertheless incapable of seeing the Grand Inquisitor as he really is. There are elements of the idealistic rationalization of power in the ideology of the Grand Inquisitor that we must overcome if we are to become fully aware of what the politics of totalitarianism come to in the end.

Clearly, that is what Orwell has in mind in the scene when Smith, while yielding more and more to O'Brien, voices the thoughts of the Grand Inquisitor only to suffer further pangs of pain for his persistence in error. Smith thinks that he will please O'Brien by explaining the Party's limitless desire for power along Dostoyevskian lines:

> That the Party did not seek power for its own ends, but only for the good of the majority. That it sought power because men in the mass were frail, cowardly creatures who could not endure liberty or face the truth, and must be ruled over and systematically deceived by others stronger than themselves. That the choice for mankind lay between freedom and happiness, and that, for the great bulk of mankind, happiness was better. That the Party was the eternal guardian of the weak, a dedicated sect doing evil that good might come, sacrificing its own happiness to that of others.

This is a fair summary of the Grand Inquisitor's ideology. O'Brien, however, has gone beyond even this last and most insidious rationalization of
power. He forcibly instructs Smith in the plain truth that "the Party seeks
power for its own sake. We are not interested in the good of others; we
are interested solely in power . . . Power is not a means; it is an end. One
does not establish a dictatorship in order to safeguard a revolution; one
makes a revolution in order to establish the dictatorship. The object of persecution is persecution. The object of torture is torture. The object of
power is power. Now do you begin to understand me?" And how does
one human being assert his power over another human being? By making
him suffer, of course. For "obedience is not enough. Unless he is suffering,
how can you be sure that he is obeying your will and not his own? Power
is in inflicting pain and humiliation. Power is in tearing human minds to
pieces and putting them together again in new shapes of your own choosing." That, precisely, is the lesson the West must learn if it is to compre-
hend the meaning of Stalinist Communism. Otherwise we shall go on playing Winston Smith, falling sooner or later into the hands of the O'Briens
of the East, who will break our bones until we scream with love for Big
Brother.

But there is one aspect of the psychology of power in which Dostoyevski's insight strikes me as being more viable than Orwell's strict realism. It
seems to me that Orwell fails to distinguish, in the behavior of O'Brien,
between psychological and objective truth. Undoubtedly it is O'Brien,
rather than Dostoyevski's Grand Inquisitor, who reveals the real nature of
total power; yet that does not settle the question of O'Brien's personal psychology, the question, that is, of his ability to live with this naked truth as
his sole support; nor is it conceivable that the party-elite to which he belongs could live with this truth for very long. Evil, far more than good,
is in need of the pseudo-religious justifications so readily provided by the
ideologies of world-salvation and compulsory happiness, ideologies gener-
ated both by the Left and the Right. Power is its own end, to be sure, but
even the Grand Inquisitors are compelled, now as always, to believe in the
fiction that their power is a means to some other end, gratifyingly noble
and supernal. Though O'Brien's realism is wholly convincing in social and
political terms, its motivation in the psychological economy of the novel
remains obscure.

Another aspect of Orwell's dreadful Utopia that might be called into
question is the role he attributes to the proletariat, a role that puts it outside politics. In Oceania the workers, known as the Proles, are assigned to
he task of production, deprived of all political rights, but unlike the Party

members, are otherwise left alone and even permitted to lead private lives in accordance with their own choice. That is an idea that appears to me to run contrary to the basic tendencies of totalitarianism. All societies of our epoch, whether authoritarian or democratic in structure, are mass-societies; and an authoritarian state built on the foundations of a mass-society could scarcely afford the luxury of allowing any class or group to evade its demand for complete control. A totalitarian-collectivist state is rigidly organized along hierarchical lines, but that very fact, so damaging to its socialist claims, necessitates the domination of all citizens, of whatever class, in the attempt to "abolish" the contradiction between its theory and practice by means of boundless demagogy and violence.

These are minor faults, however. This novel is the best antidote to the totalitarian disease that any writer has so far produced. Everyone should read it; and I recommend it particularly to those liberals who still cannot get over the political superstition that while absolute power is bad when exercised by the Right, it is in its very nature good and a boon to humanity once the Left, that is to say "our own people," takes hold of it.

1949

Postscript 1969—Orwell's novel and my review were published twenty years ago, precisely at a time when the totalitarian perversion of socialism established by the Stalinist bureaucracy in the Soviet Union appeared to us to be very secure, durable, and its horrors immitigable. None of us foresaw the disarray into which that system fell soon after Stalin's death. Still, I was able to say that *1984* should be judged primarily as a diagnosis rather than as a prognosis of things to come. I praised the book for "its powerful engagement with the present," slighting its prophetic element, and I saw clearly enough that this work, like all utopian as well as anti-utopian literature is not "aesthetically productive of ultimate or positive significance." Thus somewhat gently, to be sure, I denied it the status of a literary work of art claimed for it in certain quarters, even as in a political sense I shared its vision composed entirely, as I put it, of "images of loss, disaster, and unspeakable degradation." Also, I disagreed on psychological grounds with Orwell's notion of totalitarian power as expounded by O'Brien, the Ingsoc Commissar. Fortunately for humanity, historical events since 1949 have shown our extreme pessimism of that period, though plausible enough under the circumstances, to have been in the long run unjustified. The human mind has proven itself to be finally resistant to the methodology of terror devised by totalitarian regimes. In the last analysis, as more recent historical experience has disclosed, "Big Brother" can only earn the hatred and contempt of the Winston Smiths of this world. Happily for us, in this important matter Orwell has turned out to be quite wrong. To say that, however, is not at all to detract from the value of his novel as a timely momentous warning.

MALCOLM MUGGERIDGE

Burmese Days

George Orwell's *Burmese Days* is based, of course, on his own experiences in the Burma Police in the years after he left Eton—that is in the early twenties. There can be no doubt that this experience played a great part in his life. His family had close connections with India; he was born in Bengal, where his father was an official in the Opium Department. One day an attempt will doubtless be made, coolly and objectively, to analyse the effect on the English of their association with India. It is a fascinating subject, and whoever undertakes dealing with it will have plenty of data in works of fiction, from *Vanity Fair* to *Plain Tales from the Hills* or *A Passage to India*. *Burmese Days* belongs essentially to this tradition. It is a study of the human factor in the British Raj.

Considered simply as a novel, *Burmese Days* is not particularly satisfactory. Most of the characters are stock figures, and most of the dialogue is intended rather to present them as such than to reproduce actual conversation. The hero, Flory, is scarcely convincing, nor is the Deputy District Commissioner, Macgregor. Oddly enough, it is the villain, the fat, wicked, Burmese magistrate, U Po Sing, who best comes to life. In his portrayal there is real zest; his wickedness is presented with almost sensual delight, rather in the manner, though in a very different context, of Graham Greene.

The ordinarily-accepted view is that Orwell was deeply revolted by what was expected of him as a member of the Burma Police Force, and that his subsequent political views were to some extent a consequence of

From *World Review*, n. s. 16 (June 1950). © 1950 by *World Review*.

the great revulsion of feeling thereby induced in him. Personally, I consider that this is an oversimplification. It is perfectly true that Orwell was revolted by the brutality necessarily involved in police duties in Burma, as he was revolted by all forms of brutality, and, indeed, to a certain extent, by authority as such; but it is also true that there was a Kiplingesque side to his character which made him romanticise the Raj and its mystique.

In this connection, it is significant that one of the most vivid descriptive passages in *Burmese Days* is of the hunting expedition that Flory went on with Elizabeth. Another is of the attack on a small handful of Englishmen in their club by an enraged Burmese mob. Flory was the hero of this occasion. He, with his defacing birthmark and unorthodox attitude towards the "natives," saved the situation, whereas Verrall, "lieutenant the honourable," polo player, handsome and insolent Sahib—a sort of Steerforth as in *David Copperfield* or Townley as in *The Way of All Flesh*—unaccountably failed to put in an appearance.

These two episodes are described with tremendous gusto and vividness, and alone give promise of the considerable writer Orwell was to become. Even Flory's passion for Elizabeth, which has up to that point been difficult to believe in, comes to life when they are hunting together. Their hands meet by the warm carcase of a jungle cock—"For a moment they knelt with their hands clasped together. The sun blazed upon them and the warmth breathed out of their bodies; they seemed to be floating upon clouds of heat and joy."

On the other hand, the description of the Europeans in their club, of their discussions about electing a "native" to membership, their quarrels and their drunkenness and their outbursts of hysteria, is somehow unreal. As it happens, I was myself living in India at the same period as Orwell was in Burma. It was my first visit there. I was teaching at an Indian college in Travancore, and occasionally used to visit a neighbouring town where there was a little community of English living rather the same sort of life as the European community in Kyauktada. It is, of course, perfectly true that the general attitude towards Indians was arrogant, and sometimes brutal, and that a European who did not share this attitude was liable, like Flory, to find himself in an embarrassing situation. On the other hand, it is equally true that Orwell's picture is tremendously exaggerated, and even unreal—the sadistic outburst of Ellis, for instance:

> "If it pleases you to go to Murkhaswami's house and drink whisky with all his nigger pals, that's your look-out. Do what you like outside the Club. But by God, it's a different matter when you talk of bringing niggers in here. I suppose you'd like

little Murkhaswami for a Club member, eh? Chipping into our conversation and pawing everyone with his sweaty hands and breathing his filthy garlic breath in our faces. By God, he'd go out with my boot behind him if ever I saw his black snout inside that door. Greasy, pot-bellied little . . . !"

The fact is, it seems to me, that a tremendous struggle went on inside Orwell between one side of his character, a sort of Brushwood Boy side, which made him admire the insolence and good looks of Verrall, and a deep intellectual disapprobation of everything Verrall stood for. Verrall is presented by Orwell as, in some ways, a far more admirable character than Flory, in whom there are, unquestionably, strong autobiographical elements. Verrall is what he is; but Flory is tormented by doubt, finds his secret solace in the companionship of Dr. Murkhaswami, an Indian, and, at the same time, repeats to him gross remarks made at the club about "filthy niggers," and feels bound to sign a defamatory notice about him in connection with a proposal that he should be admitted to the club. The same conflict existed in Kipling, who, however, settled it by coming down very heavily on the Brushwood Boy side. Orwell settled it the other way, and came down heavily on the side of Paget, M. P., and "anti-imperialism." Yet, in both Kipling and Orwell the conflict really remained unresolved, leading Kipling to make the hero of his best book, *Kim*, a little English boy "gone native," and Orwell to present Verrall and U Po Sing, the two extremes of European and native callousness, as the most effective, if not the most lovable, characters in *Burmese Days*.

Orwell had an immense admiration for Kipling as a writer, though of course he deplored much of the content of his writing. His long essay on Kipling is extremely interesting, and far from being wholly denigratory. When I used sometimes to say to Orwell that he and Kipling had a great deal in common, he would laugh that curious rusty laugh of his and change the subject. One thing, incidentally, they indubitably had in common was that they found it easier to present animals than human beings in a sympathetic light; the *Jungle Books* and *Animal Farm* are cases in point. As Hugh Kingsmill remarked of Orwell, he tended only to write sympathetically about human beings when he regarded them as animals.

Burmese Days, as I have said, is not on any showing a great novel. It is, however, extremely readable and, in some of its descriptive passages, brilliant. The sense, if not the manner, of living in India is wonderfully conveyed—the boredom, the hatefulness, and, at the same time, the curious passionate glory of it. Anyone who believed that that was literally how Europeans lived in Burma before the country was "liberated," and relapsed into its present squalor and chaos and misery, would be hopelessly mistaken. There is much more to be said for British rule than Orwell says; much more that was heroic even about those little remote philistine collections of English in up-country stations than he suggests. At the same time, *Burmese Days* has its own verisimilitude, but more in relation to Orwell than to India as such.

Events have moved fast indeed since he wrote the book, and the pretentious clubs, which both U Po Sing and Dr. Murkhaswami so passionately desired to be allowed to join, have already for the most part ceased to exist, or become the haunts of brown burra Sahibs not less concerned than their white predecessors to maintain their position of superiority. If the copies of *The Tatler, The Illustrated London News,* along with local equivalents, remain where they were, and are still turned over, the Ellises, the Latimers, the Macgregors, the Westfields, have either departed, or adjusted themselves to a position of obsequiousness to their new masters. My impression was very strongly that Orwell was not quite sure how pleased he was about all this. In any case, it makes the scene of *Burmese Days* as much a period piece as Lytton's *Last Days of Pompeii.*

HERBERT READ

1984

Orwell's last work will undoubtedly rank as his greatest, though I suspect that *Animal Farm* will end by being the most popular, if only because
it can be read as a fairy-tale by children. But *1984* has a far greater range
of satirical force, and a grimness of power which could perhaps come only
from the mind of a sick man. As literature, it has certain limitations. Satire,
as Swift realised, becomes monotonous if carried too far in the same vein,
and he therefore sent Gulliver to several different countries where human
folly took on distinct guises. Though both writers have in common a sav-
agery of indignation, the comparison of their work cannot be carried very
far. Fundamental to Swift is a certain *disgust* of humanity and *despair* of
life; fundamental to Orwell is a *love* of humanity and a passionate desire
to live in freedom. There is a difference of style, too, for though both practised a direct and unaffected narrative, Swift's is still playfully baroque—
or, rather, baroquely playful. A more useful comparison is with Defoe—
and this comparison holds good for the whole of Orwell's output. Defoe
was the first writer to raise journalism to a literary art; Orwell perhaps the
last. One could make direct comparisons between their writings if it would
serve any purpose (between, say, *The Road to Wigan Pier* and the *Journal
of the Plague Year*), but I prefer an indirect comparison between *1984* and
Robinson Crusoe. The desert island is a long way from the totalitarian
State; nevertheless, there is the same practicality in the construction of
both books, and Winston Smith, "his chin nuzzled into his breast in an
effort to escape the vile wind," slipping "quickly through the glass doors

From *World Review*, n. s. 15 (June 1950). © 1950 by *World Review*.

of Victory Mansions, though not quickly enough to prevent a swirl of gritty dust from entering along with him," is the same Little Man hero who, as Robinson Crusoe, being one day at Hull, "went on board a ship bound for London . . . without any consideration of circumstances or consequences, and in an ill hour, God knows." Strictly speaking, *Robinson Crusoe* is neither a satire nor a Utopia, whereas *1984* is a Utopia in reverse—not an *Erewhon*, which is a Utopia upside-down. *Erewhon* is still written after the ameliorative pattern of *Utopia* itself: you may, paradoxically, be punished for being ill, but the ideal is health. In *1984* the pattern is malevolent; everything is for the worst in the worst of all possible worlds. But the pattern begins in the present—in our existing totalitarian States.

On page 157 there is a significant sentence which might be taken as the motif of the book: *By lack of understanding they remained sane.* The crime of Winston Smith, the hero of *1984,* was the use of a critical intelligence, his Socratic inability to stop asking questions. That "ignorance is bliss" is no new discovery, but it has generally been assumed that understanding, which brings with it a sense of responsibility, an awareness of suffering, and a tragic view of life, has compensations of a spiritual nature. It has been the object of modern tyrannies to deny man this sense of responsibility, and gradually to eliminate all feelings. The greatest enemies of the totalitarian State are not ideas (which can be dealt with dialectically) but aesthetic and erotic sensations. In the love of objective beauty, and in the love of an individual of the opposite sex, the most oppressed slave can escape to a free world. Religion is not so dangerous because it tends to be ideological and can be undermined by propaganda. But the sympathy of love, and the empathy of art—these feelings must be eradicated from the human breast if man's allegiance to Caesar (Big Brother) is to be complete. Orwell does not deal with the totalitarian hostility to art, but the dramatic quality which makes his satire so readable is due to his perception of the totalitarian hostility to love. " 'They can't get inside you,' she had said. But they could get inside you. 'What happens to you here is *for ever?'* O'Brien had said. That was a true word. There were things, your own acts, from which you could not recover. Something was killed in your breast: burnt out, cauterised out."

Orwell was a humanitarian—always moved by sympathy, by human love. The inconsistencies of his political opinions sprang from this fact. Consistently he would have been a pacifist, but he could not resist the Quixotic impulse to spring to arms in defence of the weak or oppressed. It would be difficult to say what positive political ideals were left this side of his overwhelming disillusion with Communism. In his last years he saw only the menace of the totalitarian State, and he knew he had only the force left to warn us. It is the most terrifying warning that a man has ever uttered, and its fascination derives from its veracity. Millions of people have read this book. Why? It has no charm; it makes no concession to sentiment. It is true that there are some traces of eroticism, but surely not enough to make the book, for those who seek that sort of thing, a worthwhile experience. An element of sado-masochism in the public may explain the strange success of this book. In the past the success of a book like Foxe's *Book of Martyrs* was not due to a disinterested love of the truth, or even to a hatred of Catholicism. Foxe himself was a tolerant man, but there is no evidence that his book produced a mood of tolerance in his millions of readers. I would like to think that the reading of *1984* had effectively turned the tide against the authoritarian State, but I see no evidence of it. Of Orwell's readers must it also be said: By lack of understanding they remain sane?

LIONEL TRILLING

George Orwell and the Politics
of Truth

George Orwell's *Homage to Catalonia* is one of the important documents of our time. It is a very modest book—it seems to say the least that
can be said on a subject of great magnitude. But in saying the least it says
the most. Its manifest subject is a period of the Spanish Civil War, in
which, for some months, until he was almost mortally wounded, its author
fought as a soldier in the trenches. Everyone knows that the Spanish war
was a decisive event of our epoch, everyone said so when it was being
fought, and everyone was right. But the Spanish war lies a decade and a
half behind us, and nowadays our sense of history is being destroyed by
the nature of our history—our memory is short and it grows shorter under
the rapidity of the assault of events. What once occupied all our minds and
filled the musty meeting halls with the awareness of heroism and destiny
has now become chiefly a matter for the historical scholar. George Orwell's book would make only a limited claim upon our attention if it were
nothing more than a record of personal experiences in the Spanish war.
But it is much more than this. It is a testimony to the nature of modern
political life. It is also a demonstration on the part of its author of one of
the right ways of confronting that life. Its importance is therefore of the
present moment and for years to come.

A politics which is presumed to be available to everyone is a relatively
new thing in the world. We do not yet know very much about it. Nor have
most of us been especially eager to learn. In a politics presumed to be

From *Commentary* 13, no. 3 (March 1952). © 1952 by The American Jewish Committee.

available to everyone, ideas and ideals play a great part. And those of us who set store by ideas and ideals have never been quite able to learn that just because they do have power nowadays, there is a direct connection between their power and another kind of power, the old, unabashed, cynical power of force. We are always being surprised by this. Communism's record of the use of unregenerate force was perfectly clear years ago, but many of us found it impossible to admit this because Communism spoke boldly to our love of ideas and ideals. We tried as hard as we could to believe that politics might be an idyl, only to discover that what we took to be a political pastoral was really a grim military campaign or a murderous betrayal of political allies—or that what we insisted on calling agrarianism was in actuality a new imperialism. And in the personal life what was undertaken by many good people as a moral commitment of the most disinterested kind turned out to be an engagement to an ultimate immorality. The evidence of this is to be found in a whole literary genre with which we have become familiar in the last decade, the personal confession of involvement and then of disillusionment with Communism.

Orwell's book, in one of its most significant aspects, is about disillusionment with Communism, but it is not a confession. I say this because it is one of the important positive things to say about *Homage to Catalonia,* but my saying it does not imply that I share the a priori antagonistic feelings of many people toward those books which, on the basis of experience, expose and denounce the Communist party. About such books people of liberal inclination often make uneasy and rather vindictive jokes. The jokes seem to me unfair and in bad taste. There is nothing shameful in the nature of these books. There is a good chance that the commitment to Communism was made in the first place for generous reasons, and it is certain that the revulsion was brought by more than sufficient causes. And clearly there is nothing wrong in wishing to record the painful experience and to draw conclusions from it. Nevertheless, human nature being what it is—and in the uneasy readers of such books as well as in the unhappy writers of them—it is a fact that public confession does often appear in an unfortunate light, that its moral tone is less simple and true than we might wish it to be. But the moral tone of Orwell's book is uniquely simple and true. Orwell's ascertaining of certain political facts was not the occasion for a change of heart, or for a crisis of the soul. What he learned from his experiences in Spain of course pained him very much, and it led him to change his course of conduct. But it did not destroy him, it did not, as people say, cut the ground from under him. It did not shatter his faith in what he had previously believed, nor weaken his political impulse, nor even change its direction. It produced not a moment of guilt or self-recrimination.

Perhaps this should not seem so very remarkable. Yet who can doubt that it constitutes in our time a genuine moral triumph? It suggests that Orwell was an unusual kind of man, that he had a temper of mind and heart which is now rare, although we still respond to it when we see it. About this person and the temper of his mind and heart a word ought to be said.

It happened by a curious chance that on the day I agreed to write the introduction to the new edition of *Homage to Catalonia,* and indeed at the very moment that I was reaching for the telephone to tell the publisher that I would write it, a young man, a graduate student of mine, came in to see me, the purpose of his visit being to ask what I thought about his doing an essay on George Orwell. My answer, naturally, was ready, and when I had given it and we had been amused and pleased by the coincidence, he settled down for some chat about our common subject. But I asked him not to talk about Orwell. I didn't want to dissipate in talk what ideas I had, and also I didn't want my ideas crossed with his, which were sure to be very good. So for a while we merely exchanged bibliographical information, asking each other which of Orwell's books we had read and which we owned. But then, as if he could not resist making at least one remark about Orwell himself, he said suddenly in a very simple and matter-of-fact way, "He was a virtuous man." And we sat there, agreeing at length about this statement, finding pleasure in talking about it.

It was an odd statement for a young man to make nowadays, and I suppose that what we found so interesting about it was just this oddity—its point was in its being an old-fashioned thing to say. It was archaic in its bold commitment of sentiment, and it used an archaic word in an archaic simplicity. Our pleasure was not merely literary, not just a response to the remark's being so appropriate to Orwell, in whom there was indeed a quality of an earlier day. We were glad to be able to say it about anybody. One doesn't have the opportunity very often. Not that there are not many men who are good, but there are few men who, in addition to being good, have the simplicity and sturdiness and activity which allow us to say it about them, for somehow to say that a man "is good," or even to speak of a man who "is virtuous," is not the same thing as saying, "He is a virtuous man." By some quirk of the spirit of the language, the form of that sentence brings out the primitive meaning of the word virtuous, which is not merely moral goodness, but fortitude and strength.

Orwell, by reason of the quality that permits us to say of him that he was a virtuous man, is a figure in our lives. He was not a genius, and this is one of the remarkable things about him. His not being a genius is an element of the quality that makes him what I am calling a figure.

It has been some time since we in America have had literary figures—men who live their visions as well as write them, who *are* what they write, whom we think of as standing for something as men because of what they have written in their books. They preside, as it were, over certain ideas and attitudes. Mark Twain was in this sense a figure for us, and so was William James. So too were Thoreau, and Whitman, and Henry Adams, and Henry James, although posthumously and rather uncertainly. But when in our more recent literature the writer is anything but anonymous, he is likely to be ambiguous and unsatisfactory as a figure, like Sherwood Anderson, or Mencken, or Wolfe, or Dreiser. There is something about the American character that does not take to the idea of the figure as the English character does. In this regard, the English are closer to the French than to us. Whatever the legend to the contrary, the English character is more strongly marked than ours, less reserved, less ironic, more open in its expression of wilfulness and eccentricity and cantankerousness. Its manners are cruder and bolder. It is a demonstrative character—it shows itself, even shows off. Santayana, when he visited England, quite gave up the common notion that Dickens's characters are caricatures. One can still meet an English snob so thunderingly shameless in his worship of the aristocracy, so explicit and demonstrative in his adoration, that a careful, modest, ironic American snob would be quite bewildered by him. And in modern English literature there have been many writers whose lives were demonstrations of the principles which shaped their writing. They lead us to be aware of the moral personalities that stand behind the work. The two Lawrences, different as they were, were alike in this, that they assumed the roles of their belief and acted them out on the stage of the world. In different ways this was true of Yeats, and of Shaw, and even of Wells. It is true of T. S. Eliot, for all that he has spoken against the claims of personality in literature. Even E. M. Forster, who makes so much of privacy, acts out in public the role of the private man, becoming for us the very spirit of the private life. He is not merely a writer, he is a figure.

Orwell takes his place with these men as a figure. In one degree or another they are geniuses, and he is not—if we ask what it is he stands for, what he is the figure of, the answer is: the virtue of not being a genius, of fronting the world with nothing more than one's simple, direct, undeceived intelligence, and a respect for the powers one does have, and the work one undertakes to do. We admire geniuses, we love them, but they discourage us. They are great concentrations of intellect and emotion, we feel that they have soaked up all the available power, monopolizing it and leaving none for us. We feel that if we cannot be as they, we can be nothing. Beside them we are so plain, so hopelessly threadbare. How they glitter, and with what an imperious way they seem to deal with circumstances, even when they are wrong. Lacking their patents of nobility, we might as well quit. This is what democracy has done to us, alas—told us that genius is available to anyone, that the grace of ultimate prestige may be had by anyone, that we may all be princes and potentates, or saints and visionaries and holy martyrs of the heart and mind. And then when it turns out that we are no such thing, it permits us to think that we aren't much of anything at all. In contrast with this cozening trick of democracy, how pleasant seems the old, reactionary Anglican phrase that used to drive people of democratic leanings quite wild with rage—"My station and its duties."

Orwell would very likely have loathed that phrase, but in a way he exemplifies its meaning. And it is a great relief, a fine sight, to see him doing this. His novels are good, quite good, some better than others, some of them surprising us by being so very much better than their modest genre leads us to suppose they can be, all of them worth reading; but they are clearly not the work of a great or even of a "born" novelist. In my opinion, his satire on Stalinism, *Animal Farm,* was overrated—I think people were carried away by someone's reviving systematic satire for serious political purposes. His critical essays are almost always very fine, but sometimes they do not meet the demands of their subject, as, for example, the essay on Dickens. And even when they are at their best, they seem to have become what they are chiefly by reason of the very plainness of Orwell's mind, his simple ability to look at things in a downright, undeceived way. He seems to be serving not some dashing daimon but the plain, solid Gods of the Copybook Maxims. He is not a genius—what a relief! What an encouragement. For he communicates to us the sense that what he has done any one of us could do.

Or could do if we but made up our mind to do it, if we but surrendered a little of the cant that comforts us, if for a few weeks we paid no attention to the little group with which we habitually exchange opinions, if we took our chance of being wrong or inadequate, if we looked at things simply and directly, having only in mind our intention of finding out what they really are, not the prestige of our great intellectual act of looking at them. He liberates us. He tells us that we can understand our political and social life merely by looking around us, he frees us from the need for the inside dope. He implies that our job is not to be intellectual, certainly not to be intellectual in this fashion or that, but merely to be intelligent according to our lights—he restores the old sense of the democracy of the mind, releasing us from the belief that the mind can work only in a technical, professional way and that it must work competitively. He has the effect of making us believe that we may become full members of the society of thinking men. That is why he is a figure for us.

In speaking thus of Orwell, I do not mean to imply that his birth was attended only by the Gods of the Copybook Maxims and not at all by the good fairies, or that he had no daimon. The good fairies gave him very fine, free gifts indeed. And he had a strong daimon, but it was of an old-fashioned kind and it constrained him to the paradox—for such it is in our time—of taking seriously the Gods of the Copybook Maxims and putting his gifts at their service. Orwell responded to truths of more than one kind, to the bitter, erudite truths of the modern time as well as to the older and simpler truths. He would have quite understood what Karl Jaspers means when he recommends the "decision to renounce the absolute claims of the European humanistic spirit, to think of it as a stage of development rather than the living content of faith." But he was not interested in this development. What concerned him was survival, which he connected with the old simple ideas that are often not ideas at all but beliefs, preferences, and prejudices. In the modern world these had for him the charm and audacity of newly discovered truths. Involved as so many of us are, at least in our literary lives, in a bitter metaphysics of human nature, it shocks and dismays us when Orwell speaks in praise of such things as responsibility, order in the personal life, fair play, physical courage—even of snobbery and hypocrisy because they help to shore up the crumbling ramparts of the moral life.

It is hard to find personalities in the contemporary world who are analogous to Orwell. We have to look for men who have considerable intellectual power but who are not happy in the institutionalized life of intellectuality; who have a feeling for an older and simpler time, and a guiding awareness of the ordinary life of the people, yet without any touch of the sentimental malice of populism; and a strong feeling for the commonplace; and a direct, unabashed sense of the nation, even a conscious love of it. This brings Péguy to mind, and also Chesterton, and I think that Orwell does have an affinity with these men—he was probably unaware of it—which tells us something about him. But Péguy has been dead nearly forty years, and Chesterton (it is a pity) is at the moment rather dim for us, even for Catholics. And of course Orwell's affinity with these men is limited by their Catholicism, for although Orwell admired some of the effects and attitudes of religion, he seems to have had no religious tendency in his nature, or none that went beyond what used to be called natural piety.

In some ways he seems more the contemporary of William Cobbett and William Hazlitt than of any man of our own century. Orwell's radicalism, like Cobbett's, refers to the past and to the soil. This is not uncommon nowadays in the social theory of literary men, but in Orwell's attitude there is none of the implied aspiration to aristocracy which so often marks literary agrarian theory; his feeling for the land and the past simply served to give his radicalism a conservative—a conserving—cast, which is in itself attractive, and to protect his politics from the ravages of ideology. Like Cobbett, he does not dream of a new kind of man, he is content with the old kind, and what moves him is the desire that this old kind of man should have freedom, food, and proper work. He had the passion for the literal actuality of life as it is really lived which makes Cobbett's *Rural Rides* a classic, although a forgotten one; his own *The Road to Wigan Pier* and *Down and Out in Paris and London* are in its direct line. And it is not the least interesting detail in the similarity of the two men that both had a love affair with the English language. Cobbett, the self-educated agricultural laborer and sergeant major, was said by one of his enemies to handle the language better than anyone of his time, and he wrote a first-rate handbook of grammar and rhetoric; Orwell was obsessed by the deterioration of the English language in the hands of the journalists and pundits, and nothing in his *1984* is more memorable than his creation of Newspeak.

Orwell's affinity with Hazlitt is, I suspect, of a more intimate temperamental kind, although I cannot go beyond the suspicion, for I know much less about Orwell as a person than about Hazlitt. But there is an unquestionable similarity in their intellectual temper which leads them to handle their political and literary opinions in much the same way. Hazlitt remained a Jacobin all his life, but his unshakable opinions never kept him from giving credit when it was deserved by a writer of the opposite persuasion, and not merely out of chivalry but out of respect for the truth. He was the kind of passionate democrat who could question whether democracy could possibly produce great poetry, and his essays on, say, Scott and Coleridge prepare us for Orwell on Yeats and Kipling.

The old-fashionedness of Orwell's temperament can be partly explained by the nature of his relation to his class. This was by no means simple. He came from that part of the middle class whose sense of its status is disproportionate to its income, his father having been a subordinate officer in the Civil Service of India, where Orwell was born. (The family name was Blair, and Orwell was christened Eric Hugh; he changed his name, for rather complicated reasons, when he began to write.) As a scholarship boy he attended the expensive preparatory school of which Cyril Connolly has given an account in *Enemies of Promise*. Orwell appears there as the school "rebel" and "intellectual." He was later to write of the absolute misery of the poor boy at a snobbish school. He went to Eton on a scholarship, and from Eton to Burma, where he served in the Police. He has spoken with singular honesty of the ambiguousness of his attitude in the imperialist situation. He disliked authority and the manner of its use, and he sympathized with the natives; yet at the same time he saw the need for authority and he used it, and he was often exasperated by the natives. When he returned to England on leave after five years of service, he could not bring himself to go back to Burma. It was at this time that, half voluntarily, he sank to the lower depths of poverty. This adventure in extreme privation was partly forced upon him, but partly it was undertaken to expiate the social guilt which, he felt, he had incurred in Burma. The experience seems to have done what was required of it. A year as a casual worker and vagrant had the effect of discharging Orwell's guilt, leaving him with an attitude toward the working class that was entirely affectionate and perfectly without sentimentality.

His experience of being declassed, and the effect which it had, go far toward defining the intellectual quality of Orwell and the particular work he was to do. In the 1930s the middle-class intellectuals made it a moral fashion to avow their guilt toward the lower classes and to repudiate their own class tradition. So far as this was nothing more than a moral fashion, it was a moral anomaly. And although no one can read history without being made aware of what were the grounds of this attitude, yet the personal claim to a historical guilt yields but an ambiguous principle of personal behavior, a still more ambiguous basis of thought. Orwell broke with much of what the English upper-middle class was and admired. But his clear, uncanting mind saw that, although the morality of history might come to harsh conclusions about the middle class and although the practicality of history might say that its day was over, there yet remained the considerable residue of its genuine virtues. The love of personal privacy, of order, of manners, the ideal of fairness and responsibility—these are very simple virtues indeed and they scarcely constitute perfection either of the personal or the social life. Yet they still might serve to judge the present and to control the future.

Orwell could even admire the virtues of the lower-middle class, which an intelligentsia always finds it easiest to despise. His remarkable novel,

Keep the Aspidistra Flying, is a *summa* of all the criticisms of a commercial civilization that have ever been made, and it is a detailed demonstration of the bitter and virtually hopeless plight of the lower-middle-class man. Yet it insists that to live even in this plight is not without its stubborn joy. Péguy spoke of "fathers of families, those heroes of modern life"—Orwell's novel celebrates this biological-social heroism by leading its mediocre, middle-aging poet from the depths of splenetic negation to the acknowledgment of the happiness of fatherhood, thence to an awareness of the pleasures of marriage, and of an existence which, while it does not gratify his ideal conception of himself, is nevertheless his own. There is a dim, elegiac echo of Defoe and of the early days of the middle-class ascendancy as Orwell's sad young man learns to cherish the small personal gear of life, his own bed and chairs and saucepans—his own aspidistra, the ugly, stubborn, organic emblem of survival.

We may say that it was on his affirmation of the middle-class virtues that Orwell based his criticism of the liberal intelligentsia. The characteristic error of the middle-class intellectual of modern times is his tendency to abstractness and absoluteness, his reluctance to connect idea with fact, especially with personal fact. I cannot recall that Orwell ever related his criticism to the implications of *Keep the Aspidistra Flying,* but he might have done so, for the prototypical act of the modern intellectual is his abstracting himself from the life of the family. We have yet to understand the thaumaturgical way in which we conceive of intellectuality. At least at the beginning of our intellectual careers we are like nothing so much as those young members of Indian tribes who have had a vision or a dream which confers power in exchange for the withdrawal from the ordinary life of the tribe. Or we are like the errant youngest son who is kind to some creature on his travels and receives in reward a magical object. By intellectuality we are freed from the thralldom to the familial commonplace, from the materiality and concreteness by which it exists, the hardness of the cash and the hardness of getting it, the inelegance and intractability of family things. It gives us power over intangibles, such as Beauty and Justice, and it permits us to escape the cosmic ridicule which in our youth we suppose is inevitably directed at those who take seriously the small concerns of this world, which we know to be inadequate and doomed by the very fact that it is so absurdly *conditioned*—by things, habits, local and temporary customs, and the foolish errors and solemn absurdities of the men of the past.

The gist of Orwell's criticism of the liberal intelligentsia was that they refused to understand the conditioned nature of life. He never quite puts it in this way but this is what he means. He himself knew what war and revolution were really like, what government and administration were really like. From first-hand experience he knew what Communism was. He could truly imagine what Nazism was. At a time when most intellectuals still thought of politics as a nightmare abstraction, pointing to the fearfulness of the nightmare as evidence of their sense of reality, Orwell was using the imagination of a man whose hands and eyes and whole body were part of his thinking apparatus. Shaw had insisted upon remaining sublimely unaware of the Russian actuality; Wells had pooh-poohed the threat of Hitler and had written off as anachronisms the very forces that were at the moment shaping the world—racial pride, leader-worship, religious belief, patriotism, love of war. These men had trained the political intelligence of the intelligentsia, who now, in their love of abstractions, in their wish to repudiate the anachronisms of their own emotions, could not conceive of directing upon Russia anything like the same stringency of criticism they used upon their own nation. Orwell had the simple courage to point out that the pacifists preached their doctrine under condition of the protection of the British navy, and that, against Germany and Russia, Gandhi's passive resistance would have been of no avail.

He never abated his anger against the established order. But a paradox of history had made the old British order one of the still beneficent things in the world, and it licensed the possibility of a social hope that was being frustrated and betrayed almost everywhere else. And so Orwell clung with a kind of wry, grim pride to the old ways of the last class that had ruled the old order. He must sometimes have wondered how it came about that he should be praising sportsmanship and gentlemanliness and dutifulness and physical courage. He seems to have thought, and very likely he was right, that they might come in handy as revolutionary virtues—he remarks of Rubashov, the central character of Koestler's novel *Darkness at Noon,* that he was firmer in loyalty to the revolution than certain of his comrades because he had, and they had not, a bourgeois past. Certainly the virtues he praised were those of survival, and they had fallen into disrepute in a disordered world.

Sometimes in his quarrel with the intelligentsia, Orwell seems to sound like a leader-writer for the *Times* in a routine wartime attack on the highbrows:

> The general weakening of imperialism, and to some extent of the whole British morale, that took place during the nineteen thirties, was partly the work of the left-wing intelligentsia, itself a kind of growth that sprouted from the stagnation of the Empire.

> The mentality of the English left-wing intelligentsia can be studied in half a dozen weekly and monthly papers. The immediately striking thing about all these papers is their generally negative querulous attitude, their complete lack at all times of any constructive suggestion. There is little in them except the irresponsible carping of people who have never been and never expect to be in a position of power.
>
> During the past twenty years the negative faineant outlook which has been fashionable among the English left-wingers, the sniggering of the intellectuals at patriotism and physical courage, the persistent effort to chip away at English morale and spread a hedonistic, what-do-I-get-out-of-it attitude to life, has done nothing but harm.

But he was not a leader-writer for the *Times*. He had fought in Spain and nearly died there, and on Spanish affairs his position had been the truly revolutionary one. The passages I have quoted are from his pamphlet, *The Lion and the Unicorn*, a persuasive statement of the case for socialism in Britain.

Toward the end of his life Orwell discovered another reason for his admiration of the old middle-class virtues and his criticism of the intelligentsia. Walter Bagehot used to speak of the political advantages of *stupidity*, meaning by the word a concern for one's own private material interests as a political motive which was preferable to an intellectual, theoretical interest. Orwell, it may be said, came to respect the old bourgeois virtues because they were stupid—that is, because they resisted the power of abstract ideas. And he came to love things, material possessions, for the same reason. He did not in the least become what is called "anti-intellectual," but he began to fear that the commitment to abstract ideas could be far more maleficent than the commitment to the gross materiality of property had ever been. The very stupidity of things has something human about it, something meliorative, something even liberating. Together with the stupidity of the old unthinking virtues it stands against the ultimate and absolute power which the unconditioned idea can develop. The essential point of *1984* is just this, the danger of the ultimate and absolute power which mind can develop when it frees itself from conditions, from the bondage of things and history.

But this, as I say, is a late aspect of Orwell's criticism of intellectuality. Through the greater part of his literary career his criticism was simpler and less extreme. It was as simple as this: that intellectuals did not think and that they did not really love the truth.

In 1937 Orwell went to Spain to observe the civil war and to write about it. He stayed to take part in it, joining the militia as a private. At that time each of the parties still had its own militia units, although these were in process of being absorbed into the People's Army. Because his letters of introduction were from people of a certain political group in England, the ILP, which had connections with the POUM, Orwell joined a unit of that party in Barcelona. He was not at the time sympathetic to the views of his comrades and their leaders. During the days of inter-party strife, the POUM was represented in Spain and abroad as being a Trotskyist party. In point of fact it was not, although it did join with the small Trotskyist party to oppose certain of the policies of the dominant Communist party. Orwell's own preference, at the time of his enlistment, was for the Communist party line, and because of this he looked forward to an eventual transfer to a Communist unit.

It was natural, I think, for Orwell to have been a partisan of the Communist program for the war. It recommended itself to most people on inspection by its apparent simple common sense. It proposed to fight the war without any reference to any particular political idea beyond a defense of democracy from a fascist enemy. Then, when the war was won, the political and social problems would be solved, but until the war should be won, any dissension over these problems could only weaken the united front against Franco.

Eventually Orwell came to understand that this was not the practical policy he had at first thought it to be. His reasons need not be reiterated here—he gives them with characteristic cogency and modesty in the course of his book, and under the gloomy but probably correct awareness that, the condition of Spain being what it is, even the best policies must issue in some form of dictatorship. In sum, he believed that the war was revolutionary or nothing, and that the people of Spain would not fight and die for a democracy which was admittedly a bourgeois democracy.

But Orwell's disaffection from the Communist party was not the result of a difference of opinion over whether the revolution should be instituted during the war or after it. It was the result of his discovery that the Communist party's real intention was to prevent the revolution from ever being instituted at all—"The thing for which the Communists were working was not to postpone the Spanish revolution till a more suitable time, but to make sure it never happened." The movement of events, led by the Communists, who had the prestige and the supplies of Russia, was always to the right, and all protest was quieted by the threat that the war would be lost if the ranks were broken, which in effect meant that Russian supplies would be withheld if the Communist lead was not followed. Meanwhile the war was being lost because the government more and more distrusted the non-Communist militia units, particularly those of the Anarchists. "I have described," Orwell writes, "how we were armed, or not armed, on the Aragon front. There is very little doubt that arms were deliberately withheld lest too many of them should get into the hands of the Anarchists, who would afterwards use them for a revolutionary purpose; consequently, the big Aragon offensive which would have made Franco draw back from Bilbao and possibly from Madrid, never happened."

At the end of April, after three months on the Aragon front, Orwell was sent to Barcelona on furlough. He observed the change in morale that had taken place since the days of his enlistment—Barcelona was no longer the revolutionary city it had been. The heroic days were over. The militia, which had done such heroic service at the beginning of the war, was now being denigrated in favor of the People's Army, and its members were being snubbed as seeming rather queer in their revolutionary ardor, not to say dangerous. The tone of the black market and of privilege had replaced the old idealistic puritanism of even three months earlier. Orwell observed this but drew no conclusions from it. He wanted to go to the front at Madrid, and in order to do so he would have to be transferred to the International Column, which was under the control of the Communists. He had no objection to serving in a Communist command and, indeed, had resolved to make the transfer. But he was tired and in poor health and he waited to conclude the matter until another week of his leave should be up. While he delayed, the fighting broke out in Barcelona.

In New York and in London the intelligentsia knew what had happened. The Anarchists, together with the "Trotskyist" POUM—so it was said—had been secreting great stores of arms with a view to an uprising that would force upon the government their premature desire for collectivization. And on the third of May their plans were realized when they came out into the streets and captured the Telephone Exchange, thus breaking the united front in an extreme manner and endangering the progress of the war. But Orwell in Barcelona saw nothing like this. He was under the orders of the POUM, but he was not committed to its line, and certainly not to the Anarchist line, and he was sufficiently sympathetic to the Communists to wish to join one of their units. What he saw he saw as objectively as a man might ever see anything. And what he records is now, I believe, accepted as the essential truth by everyone whose judgment is worth regarding. There were no great stores of arms cached by the Anarchists and the POUM—there was an actual shortage of arms in their ranks. But the Communist-controlled government had been building up the strength of the Civil Guard, a gendarmerie which was called "non-political" and from which workers were excluded. That there had indeed been mounting tension between the government and the dissident forces is beyond question, but the actual fighting had been touched off by acts of provocation committed by the government itself—shows of military strength, the call to all private persons to give up arms, attacks on Anarchist centers, and, as a climax, the attempt to take over the Telephone Exchange, which since the beginning of the war had been run by the Anarchists.

It would have been very difficult to learn anything of this in New York or London. Those periodicals which guided the thought of left-liberal intellectuals knew nothing of it, and had no wish to learn. As for the aftermath of the unhappy uprising, they appeared to have no knowledge of that at all. When Barcelona was again quiet—some six thousand Assault Guards were imported to quell the disturbance—Orwell returned to his old front. There he was severely wounded, shot through the neck; the bullet just missed the windpipe. After his grim hospitalization, of which he writes so lightly, he was invalided to Barcelona. He returned to find the city in process of being purged. The POUM and the Anarchists had been suppressed; the power of the workers had been broken and the police hunt was on. The jails were already full and daily becoming fuller—the most devoted fighters for Spanish freedom, men who had given up everything for the cause, were being imprisoned under the most dreadful conditions, often held incommunicado, often never to be heard of again. Orwell himself was suspect and in danger because he had belonged to a POUM regiment, and he stayed in hiding until, with the help of the British consul, he was able to escape to France. But if one searches the liberal periodicals, which have made the cause of civil liberties their own, one can find no mention of this terror. They were committed not to the fact but to the abstraction.

And to the abstraction they remained committed for a long time to come. Many are still committed to it, or nostalgically wish they could be. If only life were not so tangible, so concrete, so made up of facts that are at variance with each other; if only the things that people said were good were really good; if only the things that are pretty good were entirely good; if only politics were not a matter of power—then we should be happy to put our minds to politics, then we should consent to think!

But Orwell had never believed that the political life could be an intellectual idyl. He immediately put his mind to the politics he had experienced. He told the truth, and told it in an exemplary way, quietly, simply, with due warning to the reader that it was only one man's truth. He used no political jargon, and he made no recriminations. He made no effort to show that his heart was in the right place, or the left place. He was not interested in where his heart might be thought to be, since he knew where it was. He was interested only in telling the truth. Not very much attention was paid to his truth—*Homage to Catalonia* sold poorly in England, it had to be remaindered, it was not published in America, and the people to whom it should have said most responded to it not at all.

Its particular truth refers to events now far in the past, as in these days we reckon our past. It does not matter the less for that—this particular truth implies a general truth which, we now cannot fail to understand, will matter for a long time to come. And what matters most of all is our sense of the man who tells the truth.

PHILIP RIEFF

George Orwell
and the Post-Liberal Imagination

If there were a competition for saints in which liberals could bid, George
Orwell would be their man; he satisfies at once the liberal nostalgia for
action and their resignation to despair. Simone Weil might be another
choice. There is indeed a similarity between these two martyr figures, the
frail intellectual Jewess sickening unto death in the Renault factory and the
tired Etonian holding his own among the tramps; both made the futile gesture of going down among the "masses." But Orwell remained a self-con-
scious representative of the cultivated, and his early books are defensive
reports of his spiritual encounters in the depths of society; Simone Weil
had a different intention. Her reports are not on the practical level of the
novel or the memoir, and they have an oversubtlety that does not quite
elude the ancient religious heresy she represents which finally makes her
unacceptable not only to rationalist liberals but also to the conservative
religiosi. Orwell remains the most adequate ideal. And in a liberalism that
feels itself trapped by the Jewish question, he has the added advantage of
not being Jewish. Moreover, Simone Weil, so far as she is relevant to secu-
lar questions, is no liberal. *The Need for Roots* serves, not altogether in
agreement with her intention, the conservative polemic for a return to a
traditionalist world, while the liberal mind prefers to live in more possible
worlds. Simone Weil really looks beyond all present orders; one of
Orwell's attractions for liberals is his immersion in the here and now. He
wrote to the question of how to live in the possible world, not how to die
in an impossible one.

From *The Kenyon Review* 16, no. 1 (Winter 1954). © 1954, 1986 by Philip Rieff.

Honest living has always interested liberals more than holy dying: Orwell's problem is how to live honestly in a world that is no longer liberal, and his unique perspective on the politics and poverty of the world was gained from being very honestly involved in both. Cyril Connolly had made the basic point about Orwell's painful honesty in a biographical note on his old Eton friend in *Enemies of Promise,* and in this character Orwell has descended to us. "He was a virtuous man," writes Lionel Trilling, in his introduction to the American edition of *Homage to Catalonia;* and this was, as Mr. Trilling calls it, his "moral triumph," for Orwell's personal virtue was practiced on the basis of a decisive confusion of principle. Orwell rose above his principles and this confers upon him his peculiarly modern saintliness. He is indeed worthy of our admiration, but the aura around his nobility and courage has left the darker side—his mind—relatively unexamined. For liberals, Orwell's virtue as a man has obscured his significance as a writer. Thus Wyndham Lewis, of course not at all reverent, becomes in his recent *The Writer and the Absolute* the only critic who has treated Orwell at any length as a writer. His critical judgment, however unfair and perverse, nevertheless recognizes that Orwell is, of all "the English war and post-war writers, not alone the one most worthy of attention, but he is the only one."

The flaw in Orwell's art, Mr. Lewis thinks, lies in what he takes to be Orwell's socialist creed; only the last two popular books, *Animal Farm* and *1984,* are passable by Mr. Lewis. Liberals praise Orwell on paradoxically similar grounds: because Orwell was a socialist and because he recapitulated the liberal disillusionment with socialism. Painfully teaching themselves to accept this uncongenial world, the liberals are still troubled by a certain nostalgia for their earlier temper which finally, as socialism, sought to reject this world. But both the conservative criticism and the liberal praise of Orwell are, in his own terms, quite misplaced. The liberals had never reached socialism, and Orwell calls the earlier temper by its right name, "liberal-Christian."

"Verily," that strange accepter of all possible worlds (including Hitler's), Wyndham Lewis writes, "this man was determined to identify himself with the 'lowest of the low.' " Mr. Lewis is thinking specifically of *The Road to Wigan Pier,* Orwell's book on the coal miners. As an anti-Christian himself, Mr. Lewis thinks this is socialism. Rather, Orwell was that most liberal of liberals, the Christian who has lost his Christianity, but keeps up the essential Christian action of brotherliness and compassion. *Homage to Catalonia* opens with an expression of brotherliness and compassion, and also with the notion of its pathetic transience. George

Orwell's active and compassionate rejection of this world that describes the old liberal imagination, coupled with his sympathetic analysis of the new temper of acceptance that describes the post-liberal imagination, make him the writer most worthy of attention at least for those imaginations still in process of transition. He marked the transition more clearly than any other writer of his generation.

The first thing Orwell, as a liberal-Christian, could not accept about this world was the omnipresence of money. Rather, in his own liberal parody of religious indignation, he could not accept the omni-absence of it. Like his predecessors in the English novel of poverty from George Gissing to H. G. Wells, Orwell discovered that money was the root of all good. Money was the shield of faith that made the liberal-Christian life livable, "silky-smooth as the inside of a shell," a hard skin protecting those who had it, from the ultimate misfortune of being without it. The phrase is from Orwell's second novel, *Keep the Aspidistra Flying* (1936), and reports the suffering and resentment of the poor hero, Gordon Comstock. All of Orwell's leading characters (with the exception of Flory in *Burmese Days*) are consciously poor. It is their consciousness of their poverty that puts them in touch with reality. Poverty, the definitive experience of his heroes and one heroine, teaches them the poverty of the new world.

Orwell was stricken until death with the problem of poverty, and he made it the certain and rich theme of his writing. Poverty is as much the problem of his political tracts as of his literary criticism and fiction. Poverty connected both politics and literature. This does not contradict the fact that poverty is always treated in individual terms. The social reference, the programmatic perspective, is invariably superficial. The suggestions for reforms in hotel management and for the disposition of tramps appended to *Down and Out in London and Paris* (1931)—Orwell's first book, a memoir of a few months of his personal experience of poverty—are put forward with a curious dreamy self-consciousness, an artful childishness of statement. Poverty does not first appear in Orwell's writings as either a political or an intellectual problem. Poverty is material want. There are no myths in Orwell, and his literary manner is the English plain style. He goes directly to the point: rooming houses, vermin, sleeping under bridges, subways, cold, back alleys, orange peels, wet newspapers, hunger—all. Orwell's major aesthetic achievement is the communication of the infinite evil of not having the shield of money. There are passages in the early novels on vagrancy, on the niceties of picking through garbage, on begging and sniping, on torn clothing and compulsory camping out that are better than any others of their kind in English literature. But it is not easy to in-

terest the educated book-buying class in such matter, and Orwell's pre-war
novels were not popular. Only when he collapsed poverty into politics in
1984, did Orwell locate that vast audience with money that could not be
troubled by his original version of the politics of poverty—the simple absence of money.

The experience of poverty remained the common theme of Orwell's
fiction. It is not an experience to breathe, since one does that every minute
of one's life. Orwell is not interested in the poverty of the always poor, the
authentic proles. The Orwellian heroine and heroes have to fall into poverty. Their fall brings them what the original fall brought, knowledge of
good-and-evil. Only those whose souls have been quickened by poverty
really experience the world as it is. The experience of poverty is the loss
of innocence. Falling into poverty burdens one with a problem neither the
never poor nor the always poor suffer: quite literally, how one ought to
live.

The experience of poverty is also the loss of faith, no less than the loss
of innocence. In his first novel, *A Clergyman's Daughter* (1933), Orwell
uses the absence of money to parody the liberal-Christian loss of faith. In
a reverse conversion, Dorothy Hare loses her faith in the Christian mystery
as she learns of "the mysterious power of money." This is her liberalizing
experience. There are, indeed, three stages of the liberal imagination. The
first stage is being Christian without being liberal—action with belief. The
second stage is being liberal without being Christian—action without belief. The third stage is the post-liberal—neither action nor belief. Dorothy
moves from the first stage to the second, but rejects the invitation to move
on to the third. She can no longer take her Christianity seriously. Indeed,
the religious element in her liberalism becomes for her a private joke, one
she can't tell even her best friend. Nevertheless, Christianity remains the
incommunicable but absolute base of her liberalism, of her wish to do
good in this world.

Dorothy is reminded of a favorite joke of Mr. Warburton, the innocent, always rich man who is her would-be lover. "If you took I Corinthians,
chapter thirteen, and in every verse wrote 'money' instead of 'charity,' the
chapter has ten times as much meaning as before." Orwell thought so
much of the parody of money as the *caritas* of capitalist civilization that
he used it as the motto of his next novel, *Keep the Aspidistra Flying:*

> Though I speak with the tongues of men and of angels, and
> have not money, I am become as a sounding brass, or a tinkling
> cymbal. And though I have the gift of prophecy, and under-
> stand all mysteries, and all knowledge; and though I have all

faith, so that I could move mountains, and have not money, I am nothing. . . . Money suffereth long, and is kind; money envieth not; money vaunteth not itself, is not puffed up, doth not behave unseemly, seeketh not her own, is not easily provoked, thinketh no evil; rejoiceth not in iniquity, but rejoiceth in the truth; beareth all things, believeth all things, hopeth all things, endureth all things. . . . And now abideth faith, hope, and money, these three; but the greatest of these is money.

Orwell hammered away in all his early novels at the shield of money. "Money, once again; all is money." Money did truly exclude but one evil, poverty, as Dr. Johnson said. But this described all evil. Poverty first opened up the problem of evil as such for Dorothy Hare. Before she falls into utter poverty, she refuses to believe evil exists. By the agency of Mr. Warburton, she loses her limited Christianity and acquires a new imagination, more suited to her condition. Poverty "had driven into her a far deeper understanding than she had before of the great modern commandment—the eleventh commandment which has wiped out all the others: 'Thou shalt not lose thy job.' " The quest for certainty revealed itself in its specifically modern form, the quest for security.

A Clergyman's Daughter contains Orwell's first nightmare vision, in 1933, and it has not changed radically by *1984*. From his first novel to the last, Orwell saw "an evil time ahead." The year 1984 closely resembles 1933. In both years, Orwell describes the winter of western civilization. Both worlds are "desolate," "dank," "windless," "bleak," "colourless," "grey." The "slummy wilderness" of capitalist civilization is succeeded by the slummier wilderness of totalitarian. There are the same "labyrinths of little dingy-coloured houses," the same "derelict buildings," the same destruction everywhere. The later world is only a political translation of the earlier. What was commercial science in one has become political science in the other. Orwell first tested the great slogan of the new order ("War is Peace") in the business colleges of the old. Toots Commercial College, in the "desolate suburb" where Dorothy Hare discovers her unbelief, is in fact Orwell's first model of the garrison state. Orwell was Marxist enough to see the new society contained in the old, especially on the ideological level. The first formulation of the totalitarian catechism is contained in the advertising slogans of a business school.

Its watchword was Efficiency; meaning a tremendous parade of hustling, and the banishment of all humane studies. One of its features was a kind of catechism called the Efficiency Ritual,

which all the children were required to learn by heart as soon
as they joined the school.

Q. "What is the secret of success?"
A. "The secret of success is efficiency."
Q. "What is the test of efficiency?"
A. "The test of efficiency is success."

And so on and so on. It was said that the spectacle of the whole
school, boys and girls together, reciting the Efficiency Ritual under the leadership of the headmaster—they had this ceremony
two mornings a week instead of prayers—was most impressive.

By 1933 the prayers of Christian civilization and the slogans of capitalism were in any case indistinguishable. Both were directed to the elimination of the differences between things, or to the differentiation of identical things. Orwell simply transformed the capitalist catechism into a more
political language, but the logic was the same. Two plus two had in any
case not equalled an unequivocal four in the bourgeois arithmetic for some
time. To learn six of one is half a dozen of the other is perfect training for
the new politics. 1984 continued the shabby business accounting of 1933,
except that politics had become the world's only business. The grey dying
world of Dorothy Hare, the clergyman's daughter, ends in the grey dead
world of Winston Smith, in 1984. Winston Smith not only drinks the same
stale, weak, dirty tea of his predecessors in 1933, but his moral problem
is curiously the same: the absence of belief and the presence of poverty.
The total shabbiness of the inevitable future is Orwell's most comprehen-
sive accusation.

The acceptance of the economic catechism empties Dorothy of her
moral energy just as the acceptance of the political catechism empties Winston of his. The clergyman's daughter has been left "in a perpetually low-
spirited, jaded state, in which, try as she would, nothing seemed to interest
her. It was in the hateful ennui of this time—the corrupting ennui that lies
in wait for every modern soul—that she first came to a full understanding
of what it meant to have lost her faith." When we meet Winston Smith,
he is already jaded. He can only vaguely remember an earlier temper. He
is not at all sure just what it is he has lost. His acceptance of the meaninglessness of this world makes him happy, for the first time in his life. Her
acceptance does not make Dorothy happy, only determined. She is still too
close to the liberal-Christian temper, however exhausted it is in her, to settle passively into a world without meaning. She is too kind, and too frigid,

to be bitter; and in any case she is not an intellectual. Gordon Comstock, the thin, always hungry poet *(Keep the Aspidistra Flying),* and George Bowling, the fat insurance tout who is "thin inside" *(Coming Up for Air),* are plainly intellectuals and plainly bitter. As liberals who have not yet accepted and no longer know how to reject the meaningless world around them, they are full of the last fine activity of the liberal: imagining the utter destruction of this commercial world. From his bookshop window in 1936, Gordon Comstock

> gazed out at the graceless street. At this moment it seemed to him that in a street like this, in a town like this, every life that is lived must be meaningless and intolerable. The sense of disintegration, of decay, that is endemic in our time, was strong upon him. Somehow it was mixed up with the ad-posters opposite. He looked now with more seeing eyes at those grinning yard-wide faces. After all, there was more there than mere silliness, greed and vulgarity. . . . "Corner Table enjoys his meal with Bovex." Gordon examined the thing with the intimacy of hatred. . . . A spectacled rat-faced clerk, with patent-leather hair, sitting at a cafe table grinning over a white mug of Bovex. . . . The idiotic grinning face, like the face of a self-satisfied rat, the slick black hair, the silly spectacles. Corner Table, heir of ages; victor of Waterloo; Corner Table, modern man as his masters want him to be. A docile little porker, sitting in the money-sty, drinking Bovex. . . . He watched the ribbon of torn paper whirling, fluttering on the Q. T. Sauce advertisement. Our civilization is dying! It *must* be dying. But it isn't going to die in its bed. Presently the aeroplanes are coming. Zoom—whizz—crash! The whole western world going up in a roar of high explosives. . . . He looked at the darkened street, at the greyish reflection of his face in the pane, at the shabby figures shuffling past. Almost involuntarily he repeated: *C'est l'Ennui—l'oeil chargé d'un pleur involuntaire, Il rêve d'échafauds en fumant son houka!* Money, money! Corner Table! The humming of the aeroplanes and the crash of the bombs. . . . Gordon squinted up at the leaden sky. Those aeroplanes are coming. In imagination he saw them coming now; squadron after squadron, innumerable, darkening the sky like clouds of gnats. With his tongue he made a buzzing, blue-bottle-on-the-window-pane sound to represent the humming of the aeroplanes. It was a sound which, at that moment, he ardently desired to hear.

From his train window, after the unsuccessful attempt to come up for air, George Bowling is equally resentful. Orwell puts his unlikely George in a mood no insurance man could know, "in a kind of prophetic mood, the mood in which you foresee the end of the world and get a certain kick out of it. . . . We're all on the burning deck and nobody knows it except me. I looked at the dumb-bell faces streaming past. Like turkeys in November, I thought. Not a notion of what's coming to them. It was as if I'd got X-rays in my eyes and could see the skeletons walking. . . . I looked forward a few years." *Coming Up for Air* was published in 1939. "I saw this street as it'll be in five years' time, say, or three years' time (1941 they say it's booked for), after the fighting's started." George sees not only the burnt out buildings, but that "everyone's very thin. A platoon of soldiers comes marching up the street. They're all as thin as rakes and their boots are dragging. The sergeant's thin too and he's got a cough that almost tears him open." These are the final pages of *Coming Up for Air*. George Bowling has spanned the entire novel trying to find an escape from the money-world. He goes back to his birthplace, a village Eden of the liberal-Christian era, to inquire whether it still lives. It was a foolish question, although George does not regret spending his windfall money to find the answer, to find Lower Binfield another industrial slum. "The old life's finished, and to go about looking for it is just a waste of time. There's no way back to Lower Binfield, you can't put Jonah back into the whale." But this is only the old whale. The old world can only be recollected from the outside. George's problem is how to live inside the new whale, given the fact that "*it's all going to happen* . . . the bombs, the food-queues, the rubber truncheons, the barbed wire, the coloured shirts, the slogans, the enormous faces, the machine-guns squirting out of bedroom windows. It's all going to happen. . . . There's no escape."

Since there is no escape back into the old whale, the novel ends with George's bitter acceptance of the new. "Why had I bothered about the future and the past, seeing that the future and the past don't matter?" George decides to get back inside the new, transparent whale, passively accepting his place in it, his unbearable wife, his snotty children, the money-god, the next war—everything. He feels a certain comfort he has never felt before. Being inside the whale is, after all, the only place to be.

George Bowling's wife, like Elizabeth *(Burmese Days)*, has never revolted against the soul-defacing experience of poverty. Both women are completely hollowed out from the beginning. Some of Orwell's heroes do revolt, but the revolt ends in acceptance. George Bowling goes back to his wife and the money-world, accepting. Gordon Comstock, too, accepts the only comfort available. At the close of *Keep the Aspidistra Flying*, he has gone back to making slogans at his advertising job, and is finally seen in an ecstasy of touching all the ugly furniture in the ugly little flat in which he will begin his marriage to the world as it is. In an ecstasy of humiliation, Winston Smith finally accepts Big Brother and is really happy for the first time in his life. Poor Flory, in *Burmese Days*, cannot accept his humiliation and commits suicide. This leaves the clergyman's daughter and George Orwell himself, somewhere between acceptance and suicide, to explain themselves.

The virtue of both George Orwell and the clergyman's daughter is that they choose to remain in the middle, between a rejection made impossible by intelligence and an acceptance made impossible by morality. The old morality seems no longer defensible against the new intelligence. The liberal-Christian civilization is dead. Orwell calls the church a "powdered corpse," sweet-smelling but even more dead for that. Having put Dorothy through her education in a fine exercise in the picaresque tradition of the English novel, Orwell cannot permit her to return to any *credo non quod, sed quia absurdum est*. Orwell plainly despised those modern intellectuals who furnish their souls with what that last liberal theoretician, Max Weber, called "guaranteed genuine antiques." The Eliots and the Greenes, the Waughs and the Huxleys, are disposed of in the character of Victor, the little Anglo-Catholic lover of archaic ceremonial as against modern, in *A Clergyman's Daughter*. Weber summed up the case against the honesty of most of the intellectuals who have "returned." Their religion is simply antique collecting. They have only lost their taste for modernism or futurism. "Of all things religion is what they do not possess. By way of substitute, however, they play at decorating a sort of domestic chapel with small sacred images from all over the world, or they produce surrogates through all sorts of psychic experience to which they ascribe the dignity of mystic holiness, which they peddle in the book market." Victor peddles his religious virtuosity in the *Church Times*, but otherwise he fits Weber's description.

If Dorothy continues to go to Church, it is not as an antique dealer and certainly not out of faith rewon. "There was never a moment when the power of worship returned to her. Indeed, the whole concept of worship was meaningless to her now; her faith had vanished, utterly and irrevocably. It is a mysterious thing, the loss of faith—as mysterious as faith itself. Like faith, it is ultimately not rooted in logic; it is a change in the climate of the mind." When her intelligence makes faith impossible, Orwell has Dorothy assert "the truism that all real happenings are in the mind."

Here is Bishop Berkeley, without bringing God around to tie things together in the last chapter. It is not suffering her poverty that has made it impossible for Dorothy to return innocently to the Christian way; it is a change in the quality of her imagination. Her imagination has lost its theodical energy. She is no longer an optimist. The world can only go from bad to worse. "Something had happened in her heart, and the world was a little emptier, a little poorer from that minute." The religious coherence of intelligence and morality was no longer possible. The money-god had made all gods impossible, finally including itself, in a general exhaustion of the theodical capital built up during the Christian era.

The tension of intelligence and morality has always described the liberal imagination. Dorothy, coming at the end of the liberal-Christian era, can only understand the necessity of the connection; she can no longer make it. Having become more liberal than Christian, she can only regret that loss of faith which makes intelligence so painful. Mr. Warburton, who has intelligence without morality, as the earlier Dorothy had morality without intelligence, cannot understand Dorothy's regret. He has never been poor. He has never experienced transition, the loss of something. Instead, Mr. Warburton proclaims the new faith, Efficiency, in its present transitional, anti-political form, the efficiency of the orgasm.

But Dorothy is frigid. The irrationality of the old moral discipline has left her incapable of accepting Mr. Warburton's offer of marriage. Mr. Warburton's offer is as meaningless as his earlier attempts to seduce her. His mind is naturally impious. His is the post-liberal imagination: he not only proclaims the world meaningless but is very happy to find it so. Dorothy's terrible experience of poverty, which he had caused, means nothing to him. In fact, to the post-liberal, meaning is never a problem. Mr. Warburton is the only happy character Orwell ever describes. "The world's full of amusing things ... everything." Meaning is a moral term, to be avoided. "I've never seen any meaning in it all, and I don't want to see one. Why not take life as you find it?" But Dorothy cannot make such an acceptance. "A mind naturally pious must recoil from a world discovered to be meaningless." Dorothy recoils from Mr. Warburton, even though she knows he is correct. "Women who don't marry wither up—they wither up like aspidistras in back-parlour windows." Mr. Warburton thinks the lesson is obvious. Since the end of life is only to live, as the aspidistra has no virtue other than persistence (Gordon could not kill the one in his room, however he tried), and Dorothy's only choice is to marry or die—well then, keep the aspidistras flying.

But living is not necessarily being human. The aspidistra is not quite human. Dorothy finds it impossible to accept life for the sake of living. The human may choose to die, like Orwell himself, who might have lived had he followed his doctor's advice. Orwell's mind, like Dorothy's, was naturally pious. He belonged to the liberal-Christian era. But the liberal-Christian is very little Christian. V. S. Pritchett, in his obituary notice of Orwell, memorialized him as "a kind of saint," the "wintry conscience of a generation" (*The New Statesman*, January 28, 1950). But, as Mr. Trilling notices, Orwell's insight into the bleak age was not religious; if religion still implies some doctrine of personal sin and salvation. If for the early Dorothy everyone was innocent and all would be saved, for the late Orwell no one is guilty and none shall be saved (except perhaps the proles by their mindless sexuality).

Orwell thought he lived at the end of the liberal-Christian era, but he did not care to drive his own imagination beyond it. He thought he could discern the post-liberal imagination already, in other writers, but not in himself. He still insisted on joining morality and intelligence, as best he could. He could not accept honest sexuality as a substitute for honest social action. He thought he saw what was humanly necessary, even if it was not explainable. Orwell tried to explain Dorothy's rejection of the world as it is for her, beyond the accident of her frigidity:

> What she would have said was that though her faith had left her, she had not changed, could not change, did not want to change, the spiritual background of her mind; that her cosmos, though it seemed to her empty and meaningless, was still in a sense the Christian cosmos.

Dorothy would do her best to be a useful old maid, as before. She would meet the demands of the day, however futile they appeared. This was all that was left of her "Christian way of life." She would continue in her station, since that was her only commitment. Anyway, the church at least represented something better than what was coming. The clergyman's daughter

> perceived that in all that happens in church, however absurd and cowardly its supposed purpose may be, there is something—it is hard to define, but something of decency, of spiritual comeliness—that is not easily found in the world outside. It seemed to her that even though you no longer believe, it is better to go to church than not; better to follow in the ancient ways, than to drift in rootless freedom. . . . Just this much remained in her of the faith that had once, like the bones in a living frame, held her life together.

George Orwell was a Left Book Club man as Dorothy Hare was a Church of England girl. He remained a socialist not from belief but from disbelief in other choices. Socialism was the last form of faith of the liberal-Christian era. The socialist is then succeeded by a transitional figure: a new kind of fellow-traveler, not pink but grey, not crypto-communist but crypto-conservative, defending the good old values even as one reports their decline. These are the liberals who most appreciate Orwell.

The good old value most worth defending seems to be "plain intellectual integrity." As a liberal, Orwell is revered for nothing so much as his intellectual integrity. But intellectual integrity also points up the despair of the liberals, for it shows how meaningless the old style of questioning and searching has become. Intellectual integrity compelled Max Weber, in an essay that rattled the liberal European intelligentsia after the first world war as if it were already a skeleton, to say to those who still

> tarry for new prophets and saviors, the situation is the same as resounds in . . . Isaiah's oracles:
>
>> He calleth to me out of Seir, Watchman, what of the night? The watchman said, The morning cometh, and also the night; if ye will enquire, enquire ye; return, come.
>
> The people to whom this was said has enquired and tarried for more than two millennia, and we are shaken when we realize its fate. From this we want to draw the lesson that nothing is gained by yearning and tarrying alone, and we shall act differently. We shall set to work and meet the "demands of the day," in human relations as well as in our vocation. This, however, is plain and simple, if each finds and obeys the daimon who holds the fibers of his very life.

Orwell obeyed his daimon and met the demands of the day, in Spain and elsewhere as long as he lived. To "meet the demands of the day" is an ethic for liberals in a meaningless world. It is an ethic of action for the morally exhausted, an attempt to hold themselves and the world together.

Orwell was aware of the sources of his ethic of action. When Dorothy prays (unbelievingly) for strength, at the end of A Clergyman's Daughter, not God but "the smell of glue was the answer to her prayer. She did not reflect, consciously, that the solution to her difficulty lay in accepting the fact that there was no solution; that if one gets on with the job that lies to hand, the ultimate purpose of the job fades into insignificance; that faith

and no faith are very much the same provided one is doing what is customary, useful and acceptable." To do what is acceptable is at least to be
doing, to reject that passivity the new world is imposing upon humans.
Dorothy again begins to use herself up in her pathetically useful activities.
In the liberal theory, only the exhaustion of activity can counter the exhaustion of morality.

> The glue had liquefied. The problem of faith and no faith had
> vanished utterly from her mind. It was beginning to get dark,
> but, too busy to stop and light the lamp, she worked on, past-
> ing strip after strip of paper into place, with absorbed, with pi-
> ous concentration, in the penetrating smell of the glue-pot.

These are the final sentences of A Clergyman's Daughter. Orwell's answer
for Dorothy is his own. The only available liberal substitute for faith was
the action of gluing together what has fallen to pieces. Glue replaces Christian love as the sign of unity in the religion of the exhausted. One has to
be completely outside religious experience to conceive of religion as most
basically a mode of social cohesion. And, indeed, from Feuerbach to
Durkheim, the liberals had known faith was nothing except its function as
glue. Unity was the needful thing. (Whether it was called caritas or phallus
worship was only an accidental distinction.) It was plain to Orwell, in his
intellectual integrity, that the liberal-Christian civilization was irrevocably
exhausted, but it was necessary to act as if it were not.

Orwell saw another possibility for the exhausted. The feeling of exhaustion, so pervasive in his fiction, connects him both with the final form
of the liberal ethic and with the rise of the post-liberal imagination, exhausted beyond even the possibility of activity. Weber picked up the Efficiency theme in his despair at the growing "bureaucratization" or "rationalization" of western civilization. Orwell thought the post-liberal
imagination must accept precisely a meaningless world, accept what he
called "the deadly emptiness at the heart of things." This is the lesson "the
Warburtons of this world"—finally exemplified in O'Brien—teach the
Dorothys of this world—finally exemplified in Winston. Mr. Warburton
does not quite succeed in making Dorothy passive to the experience he offers; later tempters do succeed, and Orwell's latest hero does finally accept
and get inside the whale.

Orwell discovered his Mr. Warburton among the novelists. His name
was Henry Miller. Like Mr. Warburton, Henry Miller is that rare sight on
an Orwellian page, a happy man. Except that Miller's is American, both
men have that same "friendly voice, with no humbug in it, no moral pur-

pose, merely an implicit assumption that we are all alike." Miller is surprised that Orwell is going to Spain, and Mr. Warburton is surprised that Dorothy refuses him. But neither is overly surprised. Both take life as they find it.

Henry Miller seemed to Orwell the best literary representative yet available of the post-liberal imagination. It was not that he worshipped the meaningless, as Hindus worshipped the void. To find the world empty of meaning is still a hangover of faith; it is still a search for an answer, even a no. But Miller, Orwell discovered, asked no questions. He simply accepted the world as it is, and thus freed himself to write honestly about it.

Orwell's essay on Miller, "Inside the Whale" (1939), is a brilliant treatment of the problems of his own novels from the perspective of literary criticism. In Miller, Orwell thought he had found a writer who had gone beyond the liberal imagination instead of returning to versions before it. Miller was the most advanced novelist of this period of transition to 1984. "After all, he is a completely negative, unconstructive, amoral writer, a mere Jonah, a passive accepter of evil, a sort of Whitman among the corpses." Miller proposes the only workable ethic for the modern writer, the ethic of irresponsibility. Of course, the man has no talent. He can only publish gratuitously detailed reports on his own trivial life, quite carefree and superficial. Talent had been, in the liberal-Christian society, "being able to care." But now caring drove the writer to dishonesty. The fact that Miller cares for nothing, and suffers no beliefs lost, protects him equally against the exhaustion of those who cannot quite escape caring (Orwell thought this helped account for his own limitations as a novelist) and against the dishonesty of those who have returned to impossible answers.

Orwell explained Miller's blissful unconcern with everything happening in the world, especially with politics, as the source of his greatest literary virtue. The passage is worth quoting in full:

> War is only "peace intensified." What is quite obviously happening, war or no war, is the break-up of laissez-faire capitalism and of the liberal-Christian culture. Until recently the full implications of this were not foreseen, because it was generally imagined that Socialism could preserve and even enlarge the atmosphere of liberalism. It is now beginning to be realized how false this idea was. Almost certainly we are moving into an age of totalitarian dictatorships—an age in which freedom of thought will be at first a deadly sin and later on a meaningless abstraction. The autonomous individual is going to be stamped

out of existence. But this means that literature, in the form in which we know it, must suffer at least a temporary death. The literature of liberalism is coming to an end and the literature of totalitarianism has not yet appeared and is barely imaginable. As for the writer, he is sitting on a melting iceberg; he is merely an anachronism, a hangover from the bourgeois age, as surely doomed as the hippopotamus. Miller seems to me a man out of the common because he saw and proclaimed this fact a long while before most of his contemporaries. . . . From now onwards the all-important fact for the creative writer is going to be that this is not a writer's world. This does not mean that he cannot help to bring the new society into being, but he can take no part in the process *as a writer*. For *as a writer* he is a liberal, and what is happening is the destruction of liberalism. It seems likely, therefore, that in the remaining years of free speech any novel worth reading will follow more or less along the lines that Miller has followed—I do not mean in technique or subject-matter, but in implied outlook. The passive attitude will come back, and it will be more consciously passive than before. . . . Get inside the whale—or rather, admit that you are inside the whale (for you *are,* of course). Give yourself over to the world-process, stop fighting against it, or pretending that you control it; simply accept it, endure it, record it. . . . A novel on more positive, "constructive" lines, and not emotionally spurious, is at present very difficult to imagine.

Of course, James Joyce, Orwell thought—one might add Gertrude Stein and Virginia Woolf among others—had already muted the new anti-political literature. The Joycean novel explored "the imbecilities of the inner mind." The universal mind was an idiot, capable of nothing more than registering discrete perceptions, as in Miss Stein's famous prose poem, "One Hundred Men," "one and one and one and one" and so on to the quite arbitrary limit imposed by art. In the new literature, Orwell saw, the mind had turned in upon itself, to describe not the objects of reality but only its own perceptions. Reality was no longer a problem. Literature was to be concerned only with internal processes.

Morality, too, was no longer a problem, for it was a creation of the outer world. Only the instincts remain to the new literature as a problem, for reality and regimes are nothing to the instincts. 1984 will not abolish the instinctual life, only the coherence of morality and intelligence. This is Orwell's perverse hope for the proles, that they can live safely inside the new whale precisely because they live most closely to their instincts. The proles, Orwell thought, had never been either liberal or Christian, but sexual. They would persist in any civilization.

When Orwell wrote his essay on Henry Miller just before the war, the anti-political writers seemed in relative eclipse. But Orwell knew that soon the Eliots and the Wyndham Lewises would displace the politicals, like Auden and Spender. For one thing, they were better writers being freed, he thought, from responsibility. The only honest men were private men. The public writers of the thirties had constructed a progressive orthodoxy, and joined "movements" and "counter-movements" as if organizations could produce good fiction. But

> the atmosphere of orthodoxy is always damaging to prose, and above all it is completely ruinous to the novel, the most anarchical of all forms of literature. . . . From 1933 onwards the mental climate was increasingly against it. . . . Literature as we know it is an individual thing, demanding mental honesty and a minimum of censorship . . . a writer does well to stay out of politics.

To stay out of politics is not a protest against it, but an acceptance of whatever powers may be. "So far from protesting," Orwell writes of Miller, "he is accepting." If Miller seemed another Whitman, it only pointed up the fact that Whitman yelled "I accept" to a relatively good world; Miller yells to a bad. Miller's "mystical acceptance of the thing as it is" is an expression of the perfect amorality of the idiot mind. What Miller accepts is not "an epoch of expansion and liberty, but an epoch of fear, tyranny, and regimentation." The liberal imagination is tempted to accept even this epoch. Still trying to protect its dwindling investment in the old culture, it can always point to the constantly retreating horizon and claim rightly it is still there.

If as Orwell wrote, "the democratic vistas have ended in barbed wire," it is still the peculiar talent of many liberals to point unerringly at the breaks in the wire and at the dullness of some of the barbs. Or, the liberal may claim that the instinctual life is still free, and thus turn for the salvation of culture to anti-cultural forces. (This explains in part the enthusiastic reception of Freudianism as an ethical doctrine among liberals.) Orwell's great insight is to have insisted, rightly, that this instinctualist protest is itself a form of acceptance; and "to say 'I accept' in an age like our own is to say that you accept concentration camps, rubber truncheons, Hitler, Stalin, bombs, aeroplanes, tinned food, machine guns, putsches, purges, slogans, Bedaux belts, gas masks, submarines, spies, provocateurs, press censorship, secret prisons, aspirins, Hollywood films, and political murders." No doubt "on the whole this is Henry Miller's attitude." At least, it is more honest than the corrupting optimism that says: "Not *only* these things, of course."

The liberal imagination at the end of its optimism is deeply irritable; it would feel better if the whole civilization blew up. Gordon Comstock and George Bowling are always imagining that probability, and here Orwell himself was very close to Henry Miller's temper. He, as Orwell notices sympathetically, is always talking about blowing the place up. (Rejection has become a fantasy.) Orwell is mistaken, however, to think that Miller's autobiographical technique and subject-matter are only accidental to his posture of acceptance. Miller's concern with sex is no more accidental to him than it was to Mr. Warburton. If "Miller is simply a hard-boiled person talking about life, an ordinary American business-man with intellectual courage and a gift for words," sex is Henry Miller's business, and the only really worthwhile racket. It is not exile that made Miller write about "the man in the street full of brothels—of people drinking, talking, meditating and fornicating, not about people working, marrying and bringing up children." Nor, as Orwell thinks, could Miller "describe the one set of activities as well as the other." It is not exile but honesty, not the penalty of leaving your native land and thus necessarily transferring your roots to shallower soil. Rather, all soil has become shallow. As for one's roots, the thing is to be allowed to dig them up; and Miller found that easier to do in Paris than in New York.

Like Orwell, Miller had the experience of poverty; both had been down and out in Paris. Their descriptions of this experience could not be more antithetical. But still Orwell is sympathetic to Miller, even to the point of misunderstanding the necessities of his art, narrowing the gap between the liberal and the transitional writer. It is not so important that Orwell misunderstood Miller, out of sympathy for the common predicament of modern writers, but that he is sympathetic. His sympathy marks the loosening of his imagination from its old liberal forms.

Perhaps it is worth recalling liberals to the traditionally pejorative understanding of the term "imagination." Until the dawn of romanticism in the late eighteenth century, imagination had always been considered a source of error; and it is still true that, as an aesthetic term, "imagination" connotes moral and intellectual permissiveness. Creativity undisciplined by morality and reason is still a dangerous possibility, breaking through the forms in which it must be limited to be art. But Orwell does not consider

Miller's art critically. In the final exhaustion of the liberal imagination, it is possible to treat a writer who is neither liberal—Miller, Orwell proclaims, is happily free of moral sensibilities—nor imaginative—Miller's perceptions are as superficial as his subject-matter—as representative of the only creative possibility in modern literature.

What drives the liberal imagination beyond itself is precisely the ascendancy of imagination, no longer confident in its liberal-Christian forms. Orwell was the perfect liberal, neither passive nor unimaginative. Yet at the same time there was in Orwell a residual ambiguity typical of the finest liberalism. The sympathetic acceptance of the acceptor of 1984, along with the acutest picture of what 1984 would really be like, is a *caritas* liberalism cannot afford to pay for the sake of improving its imagination.

RICHARD WOLLHEIM

Orwell Reconsidered

The reissue of a book twenty-odd years after its original appearance makes some of the conventions and courtesies of reviewing superfluous. Once it has come of age a book should be judged by the standards of history. Judged by these standards *The Road to Wigan Pier* is undoubtedly a piece of out-of-date journalism. Let us consider each of these charges separately.

The charge of journalism is one made freely in general criticism, and we should make an effort to use it sparingly and with precision. What makes *The Road to Wigan Pier* a piece of journalism isn't its content, nor the urgency with which it is written, nor even exactly its style. It is, rather, the particular attitude that the author adopts toward his subject matter. Whether he is writing about the condition of the working classes in the 1930s (as in the first part of the book) or about the predicament of socialism and socialists (as in the second part), his method is the same. In each case, what he does is to pick out from the material at his disposal a number of details all of them as startling, as shocking, as arresting as possible, and then to set them down in a style that is very deliberately and very self-consciously none of these things. The method is undoubtedly effective. One would have to be very thick-skinned indeed not to be deeply discomforted by *The Road to Wigan Pier*. But the method has also its defects, and the most important of these is that it tends to distortion. Such a tendency is most evident in the second or argumentative part of the book where Orwell in his desire to make every point count for one, succeeds often

From *Partisan Review* 27, no. 1 (Winter 1960). © 1960 by Partisan Review, Inc.

enough in completely obliterating the lines of the discussion. One feels that
a man could not be so interested in stressing the persuasive or emotive elements in a thesis unless he believed in it; and then it turns out that Orwell
doesn't. But it would be uncharitable to dwell too long on Orwell's defects
as a theoretical writer. For he in this matter is the chief loser: even now it
seems as likely as not that he will be remembered for ideas that, even if he
did propound them at some length and with some vehemence, certainly
aren't his. But this same passion for the striking and strident detail, for
anything that catches the eye or plays on the nerves, is also Orwell's undo-
ing as a descriptive writer. There is much in *The Road to Wigan Pier* that
must be amongst the ineradicably painful memories of any sensitive
reader: the inferno of the miners at the hour when the "fillers" are working the coal face; the old age pensioners driven from their homes by the
means tests and dying wretchedly in lodging-houses; the newspaper canvassers keeping down their miserable jobs until they are worn out by the
helplessness of the work; the Brookers' tripe shop, and the beetles, and
Mrs. Brooker wiping her greasy mouth on strips of newspaper. But the ac-
cumulation of these sharp, stabbing pictures doesn't seem to add up to a
vision of the whole: what we are left with is a series of stills, mostly "close-
ups," which no one has animated. We learn from Orwell a great deal
about what, twenty-three years ago in Wigan or Sheffield, one would have
seen, or heard, or smelt, but what one gets singularly little idea of is what
it would have been like to have lived there.

Now I know that this—particularly this last sentence—sounds like the
usual kind of "literary criticism" that is bestowed in a bland way on any
genuine work of social protest. Moreover in this case it isn't exactly criticism. For is it not part of Orwell's own thesis that in a modern industrial
society it is quite impossible for one half of the community, even with the
best will in the world, to arrive at anything like a proper understanding of
how "the other half" lives? This has nothing to do with class-warfare or
class hatred: it is simply a matter of class-*difference*. The two "halves" live
in such entirely different ways that language cannot bring them together.
It is as if there were certain things in life which are so important in themselves and so far-reaching in their consequences that if one doesn't know
them directly, by acquaintance, one is never going to obtain knowledge of
them by description.

And yet I think there is something in Orwell's style or manner that
does exacerbate this problem for him, and it is what I have called his
journalism. To see what I mean, you have only to compare *The Road to
Wigan Pier* with another book about modern poverty: Carlo Levi's *Christ*

Stopped at Eboli. Levi also has taken for his subject people who simply by virtue of the physical conditions of their existence have placed themselves beyond the understanding of the educated. Indeed of the two those about whom Levi writes are poorer, more backward, more isolated from and ignorant of modern concerns and interests, and yet I think that at the end of his book one knows—I don't just mean that one has the *feeling* or *sensation* of knowing, but that one actually *knows*—more about the half-starved superstitious peasants of Lucania than one does after reading Orwell about the unemployed of Wigan. And the reason for this is, quite simply, that whereas one book is a work of journalism, the other is a work of literature: not high literature perhaps, but literature.

From the very beginning the difference is evident. Levi starts from a position that is somewhat back from his subject, and it is only slowly, gradually that he works his way towards, and then into, it: all the while bringing his reader with him, neither dragging behind him nor rushing ahead. Where Orwell is knowing, Levi is informative. He takes nothing for granted: he even tells one on the first page of the book what the word *"christiano"* means in the usage of the uneducated, which is something that an alert tourist to Italy can pick up for himself. But when he explains something, he does so as, one feels, the peasants he is writing about would if they could: when, for instance, he recounts the strange beliefs that the peasants hold about wolves and gnomes, it is only external evidence that tells one that these beliefs aren't also his. On the other hand, when Orwell tells one something about what his working-class people think or feel— and it is amazing how rarely he refers to anything except the physical terms of their life—he does so in a way that is striking but *external:* he reminds one forcefully that it is a necessary truth that one can only ever see the surface of things.

Perhaps the greatest difference between the two writers is that Orwell subscribes to, and is guilty of, the great fallacy of naturalism: the belief that the essence of the things in time can be conveyed by reference to the transient and the ephemeral. It is easy enough to believe this. It is easy enough to think that if you mention the P.A.C. and Worcester sauce and Carnera and lounge lizards, then you have forever conveyed the feel of 1936. It is easy enough to think this when you write it, and easy enough to go on thinking it when a few months later you read the proofs of what you have written. It is only the reader reading it twenty years later who has his doubts, and twenty years further on those doubts are confirmed when the book is read either by people with "special interest" in the period or by no one at all. Perhaps Orwell would have thought that this didn't matter: perhaps he would have thought that he wrote in the first place for his own contemporaries, and that if by any chance someone at a later date wanted to read him, so much the better, but this wasn't in the calculation. Orwell, I say, might have thought this, but I doubt if in all honesty he did. Because I think that ever since the concept of literature was invented, these have not been the thoughts of writers.

The matter may be put like this: Orwell, I suggested, addresses himself primarily to the eye and the nerves. It is this that marks him out as a journalist, and good or honest journalists are distinguished from bad or dishonest journalists by the fact that they would not pretend to be appealing elsewhere. The limitation of the method is that two areas of the human constitution toward which literature is traditionally directed are ignored: the head and the heart. By contrast *Christ Stopped at Eboli* in its quiet, gentle, unpretentious way never leaves either of these two areas untaxed or unaddressed for long. That is what makes it a moving book: while *The Road to Wigan Pier* is at its best a maddening one: a book to send one mad with rage and indignation and shame.

And that of course is its aim. Orwell in writing *The Road to Wigan Pier* was writing a polemical book whatever else he was also writing. He wanted to draw people's attention to the conditions of the day: and he felt that it was urgently necessary to do this, not just because of the conditions themselves, but because of a further belief he entertained with great conviction about the immediate future of the world. This belief was in fact false and the conditions to which Orwell wanted to draw attention are no longer what they were. And this is why I describe *The Road to Wigan Pier* as not just journalism but also out-of-date journalism.

The belief in the light of which Orwell reviewed the state of England was that there were two and only two possible political futures for the world: Socialism and Fascism. There was perhaps a great deal in the contemporary scene that obscured and complicated the picture and prevented one from seeing this simple fact: but soon enough the fog of ideology and party would clear and it would become evident beyond all doubt that in the coming struggle for power there were only two entrants. Today this certainly is not the case. Whether it was ever reasonable to think this is another matter. Nor should it concern us much, for it seems to have been a peculiar feature of the 1930s that the rationality of a man's political prognostications varied inversely with his intelligence—*vide* supremely Keynes's interpretation of the Munich Settlement in the *New Statesman*. Anyhow it is quite clear that the future is not for us as Orwell envisaged it.

Nor are the conditions of England on which he rested his gaze recognizably the same. In Orwell's England there were two million unemployed: In June 1958 there were 472,000—and 1958 was, of course, a bad year compared with 1957 and 1956 when there were 297,000 and 250,000 respectively. In Orwell's England a man on public assistance drew (roughly) 12/6 for himself, another 12/6 for his wife, 4/– for his oldest child and 3/– for any other child: so that an average family subsisting on the dole had about 30/– on which to live. Today a man gets 53/– for himself, another 30/– for his wife, 15/– for his eldest child and 7/– for any other child: in addition he gets 8/– family allowance for any child (except the first) who is still at school, so that the father of a family has an income of about £5-10-0. Against this we must offset a rise in the standard of living of about 200%, but this still means an appreciable increase in real terms: i.e., £5-10-0 as against an equivalent of £4-10-0, or a rise of 20%. Again Orwell concentrated a great deal on conditions in the coal mines, and here of course the changes have been more spectacular. The average earnings per shift for all mine-workers is given by Orwell as 9/1¾d: in 1957 it was 57/2d—a rise even in real terms of over 100%. The average earnings of a miner per week in Orwell's England was £2-2-0: the comparable figure for 1957 is £14-10-4d—a rise of about 130%. Along with this increase in wages there has gone a no less remarkable improvement in welfare, in the social and industrial conditions of the miner. The fatal accident rate, for instance, on which Orwell lays considerable stress has halved between then and now. The truth is that the mining industry from being one of the most backward and poverty-stricken areas of the national economy has become, in what is perhaps its ultimate phase, one of the most prosperous and progressive.

This is not to say that in the England of today, in the British Welfare State, hardship and misery are unknown. There is a great deal of both. But neither is to be found where Orwell found them; in location, and perhaps even more in character, they have changed. The poverty of today is "secondary" rather than "primary"; it affects the old and the sick, the neglected and the improvident, the lame ducks of the class system and not, as in Orwell's day, the centrally-placed members of one specific class. And though inequality is as much a feature of our England as of his, the whole structure of inequality has been shifted upwards, en bloc as it were, so that today its evil effects are not recognizably what they were, being cultural and psychological rather than anything material in the crude sense. The evils of contemporary Britain are not those of insufficiency but of injustice; and though Orwell talked of injustice, what he was really interested in doing was to point out to those who had enough to eat that there were others living not a hundred miles away who hadn't. And yet it must be said in all fairness to Orwell that the kind of remedy we need for our ills did not fall outside his imaginative grasp.

The Road to Wigan Pier is then a piece of out-of-date journalism. It is, if I am not wrong, out-of-date and it is journalism. But is it anything else as well? In answering this question I want to avoid a larger question that enjoys a certain vogue in England at the moment and in which it would be only too easy to get immersed: that is, Orwell as a case. This larger question arises from considering all of Orwell's books together, the books he wrote against the future as well as those he wrote against the present, both Animal Farm and 1984, on the one hand, and Down and Out in Paris and London and The Road to Wigan Pier, on the other hand, and then asking whether the earlier books lead on to the later books and where the later books lead, if, that is, they lead anywhere at all.

But whatever we make of the larger question I am certain what answer we should give to the narrower question. Of course The Road to Wigan Pier is more than its defects. More specifically, its merit resides in the question that it raises and round which, in its fluid way, the book is centered. The answers that Orwell gives to his question are seldom interesting and sometimes downright silly. Even at his best Orwell suffered from two failings which stood in the way of his being much of a thinker; he was too argumentative, and he was too forgetful. Too argumentative, in that when he could not make up his mind on the merits of an issue he preferred to take both sides, each against the other. Too forgetful, in that he often seems to have been quite unable to remember on one page what he wrote on another. But, as I say, the merit of The Road to Wigan Pier, what saves it from the scrap heap, is the question that it poses; and that question might be rendered as, What is it really to be a Socialist?

Now it is nowadays held to be one sign of philosophical naïveté to ask questions of the form, What is a real x? or What is it really to be an x? For, the argument runs, any such form of words serves to conflate, and hence to confuse, two very different issues that might be raised. One is the verbal, often trivial issue, What is the meaning, or definition, of x? and the other is the normative or ethical question, which can be formulated more satisfactorily as, What ought an x to be like? or, What is a good x? Now these two questions, the verbal and the ethical, are evidently different, and if proof is required of this it lies in the fact that no answer to a question of the first kind could be an answer to a question of the second kind. For if it could be, then it would be possible to rule out by definition the possibility of an x's being what it oughtn't to be, or, more simply, of a bad x: which is an evident absurdity.

Now it is no part of my case to defend Orwell from a charge of philosophical naïveté. But, after all, it is I, not Orwell, who formulated the question in this seemingly objectionable way, and since I have argued that the case for *The Road to Wigan Pier* hangs on this question, it is undeniably my task to explain what I understand by it.

We might put it like this: A certain number of people (perhaps ourselves included) are in the habit of describing themselves as socialists. At elections there is every reason to believe that they vote for a Socialist candidate or the nearest thing they can find. The question now arises, over and above voting Socialist—and, of course saying that they are socialists—what makes them socialists? Or are these two things enough? Do they by themselves constitute a belief in socialism? If they do, then a belief in socialism seems to be, in the first place, something easy to come by, and, secondly, curiously unconnected with the great practical problems to which socialism is supposed to relate. But, then, if these things do not constitute a belief in socialism, what more is required?

The question is a salutary one. As the barest minimum it must have the following effect on anyone who considers it at all seriously: that either he will require more of someone before he regards him as a socialist, or he will attach rather less weight to the assignment of political belief. It was characteristic of the thirties, at any rate in England, that they at one and the same time distributed political labels (both honorific and pejorative) with greater liberality than had traditionally been the case, and also set greater store by these labels. Orwell was, if anyone ever was, a child of his age, but in posing what I have called the central problem of *The Road to Wigan Pier* he provided a solvent for some of the worst superstitions of his contemporaries.

Orwell's concern is, then, not so much with socialism as with Belief. The first question a socialist must ask himself is: If I believe in *socialism*, what is it that I believe in? And there must be few socialists who don't ask themselves this question. But the second question that a socialist should ask himself is one that I suspect very few socialists do. It is: If I *believe in* socialism, how do I stand to socialism? And that is Orwell's question. What made him raise it?

In *The Road to Wigan Pier* Orwell describes his own road to socialism, and I think that if we consider this more closely we shall find our answer. When Orwell left Eton—a word he won't quite mention—he joined the Indian Imperial Police and went to Burma. He was there for five years, administering a rule that he gradually came to feel was absolutely unjustifiable. It was, in his eyes, quite simply a system of oppression, and by helping to sustain it he himself was an oppressor. When he came back to England on leave in 1927, he could bear it no longer: he threw up his job and never went back. "I was not going back to be a part of that evil despotism" is how he puts it. But once back in England he could not feel free of the charge of being an oppressor. For the working classes of England, it now occurred to him, were just as much victims of injustice as the unfortunate Burmese. Indeed the system of oppression in Britain of one class over another seemed, if anything, worse because harsher and less tempered with mercy than the more publicized system that existed outside Britain of one country over another. The question then arose for Orwell, How could he contract out of the second system as he had out of the first? What in the case of capitalism was the analogue of leaving the Indian Imperial Police? The obvious answer was socialism. But what did socialism involve? If it was no more than a theoretical belief, then to embrace socialism was the exact counterpart of declaring oneself to be a little Englander and staying on in the Indian Imperial Police. Surely there must be something more— and this, of course, is how the central problem of *The Road to Wigan Pier* came to assert itself.

The "sensible" answer to Orwell's question is, I suppose, that there is no analogue to leaving the Indian Imperial Police. There is no single action or set of actions that counts as contracting out of the capitalist system. Of course there may be at different times different things one can do—but there is, as it were, no standing action for someone who rejects capitalism. And that is because capitalism is a pervasive system in a way which imperialism isn't. In part the point is a purely formal one: it derives from the fact that we call everything in a capitalist system "capitalism" though a great deal of it may be quite unconnected with the undesirable aspects of the system and indeed would probably be exactly as it is under any system. In part the point is not formal: in a capitalist society the institutions of capitalism are strategically placed and they contrive in varying degrees to color and affect most of what happens throughout the society. But however we look at the problem, the answer is the same. There is no way of washing one's hands of capitalism. And by this I don't just mean that one person's contracting out of the system isn't going to make such a difference or isn't going to bring the system to an end. I mean that there is no method of contracting out of the system. The person who rejects capitalism is in a position closer to that of the pacificist than to that of the vegetarian.

Of course there will always be people who won't accept the "sensible" answer. Even if one can't get outside the system, they argue, one can at any rate work oneself very close to the periphery, and it is too convenient and easygoing an answer to say that because one can't hope for total success, therefore one shouldn't try at all. The thing is like a stain: one may not be able to remove it, but one can at least get it paler.

Certainly this is what Orwell felt, and it would be hard—particularly for anyone who has no intention of following him—not to admire him for it. What he proved to himself, and proved for the benefit of anyone who cares to learn, is that a great deal of what is clung to in bourgeois life, is clung to not on account of the pleasure it gives but out of the fear of giving it up. The pleasures of the rich should occupy a place of respect in the thoughts of any genuine reformer: if only for the good utilitarian reason that the rich get pleasure from them. But the so-called "pleasures" of the rich from which none get pleasure and for the sake of which many suffer, deserve no mercy from anyone; and it is one of the great merits of a modern Thoreau like Orwell that he shows these things up for what they are.

It is, then, impossible not to admire Orwell for his attempt to detach himself from bourgeois life and to effect a total immersion in the life of the working classes. As an act of renunciation and penance it has a heroic quality; it sets him aside as one kind of superior person, the kind that does things that others can't get themselves to do. But there comes a point in Orwell's writing when the act ceases to have a purely personal or even penitential character, and the life of the working classes is presented not just as a life we should all know about nor as the only life a free man can lead, but as a definitely superior condition, as a form of existence that, quite apart from considerations of curiosity or conscience, it would be reasonable to prefer to anything else that modern life has to offer:

> Curiously enough it is *not* the triumphs of modern engineering, nor the radio, nor the cinematograph, nor the five thousand novels which are published yearly, nor the crowds at Ascot and the Eton and Harrow match, but the memory of working-class interiors—especially as I saw them in my childhood before the war, when England was still prosperous—that reminds me that our age has not been altogether a bad one to live in.

The passage taken as a whole seems to me to be as good an example as one could find of the sort of slovenly emotive writing that in other quarters Orwell thought it his duty to scourge. Why, for instance, does he suppose that the aspects of life he opposes to working-class life are the only other candidates for excellence? Or why does he suggest that those who support middle-class culture do so on account of any of these things? Still, Orwell's championship of proletarian culture, stripped of its false rhetoric, is of considerable interest; not least because of its parallelism with a cultural movement in English thought today.

The most notable feature of Orwell's case is that he produces no coherent evidence in its favor. On the contrary everything he says in the ordinary course of description about working-class life seems designed to turn one against it. It may make people—at any rate those with strong enough defenses—kinder, gentler, nicer, but only in the way in which being adrift on a raft is supposed to bring out the best in people: because of its awfulness. Just before the passage I have quoted, Orwell attempts some sort of eulogy of working-class family life, but in doing so it is noticeable that he falls into the crudest kind of sentimentality:

> Especially on winter evenings after tea, when the fire glows in the open range and dances mirrored in the steel fender, when Father, in shirt-sleeves, sits in the rocking chair on one side of the fire reading the racing finals, and Mother sits on the other with her sewing, and the children are happy with a pennorth of mint humbugs, and the dog lolls roasting himself on the rag mat—it is a good place to be in.

And when Orwell pulls himself out of sentimentality, it is only to take refuge in a preciosity that is no less disagreeable: the scene described above he praises as exemplifying "the perfect symmetry as it were of a working-class family at its best."

The other point about Orwell's championship of proletarian culture is the difficulty of reconciling it with his socialism. For if working-class culture is all that superior, it is hard to see why it ought not to be retained: yet, equally, it is hard to see how it can be retained, if one abolishes the material conditions on which it must to some extent at least depend. Orwell—who was never a man to pass over situations that were awkward for his views, though he did not always see their full implications—deals with this problem when he considers the rehousing of some of the slum inhabitants of Wigan. The rehousing Orwell regarded as a monstrosity: it was "ruthless and soulless." The new inhabitants had been taken out of their old homes, removed from their friends, their shops, their pub, and put down in a bleak inhospitable estate, miles from where they worked, with no centre of social life, where they weren't even allowed to do many of the things they most wanted to, such as keeping pigeons. Of course Orwell admits in the end that the change *is* a change for the better, but by now it is obscure to see how it can be so on his view of the matter. Nowadays, as I mentioned earlier, there is a school of thought that tries to combine anew Orwell's political and cultural predilections. The most persuasive, in any case the most poignant, expression of this point of view is in Richard Hoggart's *The Uses of Literacy,* and it finds a recurrent echo in the lively pages of *The University and Left Review.* If this school of thought is ever to progress beyond a kind of antiquarianism, it must try to resolve what looks like an inherent paradox in its thinking. For traditionally nearly all socialism, indeed nearly all reformism, accepts to some extent at least a theory of the dependence of cultural on material conditions: it is difficult to see where it would draw its inspiration from if it totally abandoned any such conception. And yet if it does adhere to such a conception, it is hard to see how it can envisage and advocate as the working-class future thorough-going reform in the material field along with total conservatism in the field of culture. The workers, it seems to suggest, have only their chains to lose: for everything that goes with their chains they must preserve.

It is no part of my case to suggest that a critic of working-class conditions ought to believe in the superiority of bourgeois culture, or that it is unreasonable to feel concern about the extent to which socialism in practice has come to mean the progressive assimilation of the more intelligent members of the working class into the middle class. My real point is that it is unnecessary for a socialist to have any very strong or precise views about the kind of culture that a socialist society should incorporate: and not merely unnecessary but unwise. A common argument used by thinkers of a reactionary kind is that a certain earlier period of history, say the Middle Ages, was not inferior to the present because the people who lived then were not evidently or articulately discontented with their circumstances. To this argument the evident retort is that they weren't discontented because they didn't know better: whereas people who live nowadays and have some knowledge of both forms of culture wouldn't revert. The principle of the argument is this: that cultural preferences are of interest only if they are expressed between cultures both of which are known or familiar. And the principle has relevance for those interested in the future of society. With what right do we try to impose upon some yet unborn society some existing form of culture when most likely a new form will arrive of its own accord which may well be preferable to anything we can envisage? The proper field for "reformism" is material conditions, for here the consequences of any move we make are more or less ascertainable and their desirability or otherwise a suitable matter for the informed moral judgment.

To Orwell such an attitude was repugnant. "To take a rational political decision," he was to write in his essay on Koestler, "one must have a picture of the future." Of course to some extent one must: but not, I maintain, a picture possessed of that degree of detail which Orwell thought necessary. And I think that he pitched his demands so high for two reasons neither of which is valid. In the first place, as we have seen, he believed that the only *practical* political alternative to socialism was fascism, and fascism had a picture of the future, and therefore if one wanted to beat fascism one must have a bigger and brighter picture. In other words, Orwell anticipated an argument of which, *mutatis mutandis,* we have heard enough and more than enough during the Cold War. The other reason why Orwell thought that socialism required a complete vision of the end towards which it was directed is, I suspect, that fundamentally he believed in conformity. To some the appeal of socialism resides in the fact that it holds out the prospect of a society, to be realized at some not too distant date in the future, in which men, all of them, will be free to lead the life they choose. Without in any way rejecting this ideal of autonomy Orwell makes it fairly clear that for him the attractions of socialism are not derivative from it. What he looked for in socialism was the inauguration of a certain determinate way of life: a "decent" way of life—to use a favorite expression of his. It is true that Orwell gives as one of the "essential aims" of socialism *liberty*—the other one being *justice*—but to Orwell (who here as elsewhere has so much in common with Rousseau) liberty meant not the ability to lead whatever kind of life one might choose, but rather a particular quality, or characteristic, pertaining to the kind of life he expected everyone to choose. Liberty in Orwell's scheme of things finds its natural contrast in servility rather than in constraint. It would be no great parody of Orwell to say that for him a free society was a society in which no man touched his cap to another. Yet it is quite clear that in such a society, a society of hard, proud, self-reliant, manly men, there could be a terrible absence of liberty as we ordinarily think of it. What Orwell hated were things like bureaucracy and pomp and Five Year Plans and restrictions and propaganda: these things he thought, and rightly thought, incompatible with liberty. But what he seems also to have hated is crankiness, affectation, perversion, "softness," aestheticism: and I don't think that he would have regarded it as any great breach of liberty to crowd these things out of society—not to suppress them, mind you, but to crowd them out, to sweep them under the carpet. And there I'm sure he was wrong.

But I do not want to end on a note of criticism. The limitations of *The Road to Wigan Pier* are very much the limitations of the age. The book was written, we must remember, in an epoch when it was held that all literature should aspire to the condition of journalism. And it must be said in Orwell's favor that out of this dusty program he managed to snatch a success well beyond the reach of any of his English contemporaries. One has only to compare *The Road to Wigan Pier* with another typical product of the age with which it has marked affinities—Grierson's documentary films—to be struck by the direct and humane and unpretentious nature of Orwell's writing. And in one passage, at least, the book transcends the limitations that the author imposed upon it: sincerity, passion, and observation suddenly combine to produce a fragment of true literature. Orwell is leaving Wigan. He looks out of the train, and as we listen to his description of the scene, we hear, unexpectedly (but all the more moving for that), the note of true poetry: the elegiac poetry of the modern city, the poetry created by Baudelaire and the Goncourts, and transplanted and refashioned by the young Joyce:

> This was March, but the weather had been horribly cold and everywhere there were mounds of blackened snow. As we moved slowly through the outskirts of the town we passed row after row of little grey slum houses running at right angles to the embankment. At the back of one of the houses a young woman was kneeling on the stones, poking a stick up the leaden wastepipe which ran from the sink inside and which I suppose was blocked. I had time to see everything about her— her sacking apron, her clumsy clogs, her arms reddened by the cold. She looked up as the train passed, and I was almost near enough to catch her eye. She had a round pale face, the usual exhausted face of the slum girl who is twenty-five and looks forty, thanks to miscarriages and drudgery; and it wore, for the second in which I saw it, the most desolate, hopeless expression I have ever seen. It struck me then that we are mistaken when we say that "It isn't the same for them as it would be for us," and that people bred in the slums can imagine nothing but the slums. For what I saw in her face was not the ignorant suffering of an animal. She knew well enough what was happening to her—understood as well as I did how dreadful a destiny it was to be kneeling there in the bitter cold, on the slimy stones of a slum backyard, poking a stick up a foul drainpipe.

NICHOLAS GUILD

In Dubious Battle: George Orwell
and the Victory of the Money-God

When Gordon Comstock, the moth-eaten hero of George Orwell's *Keep the Aspidistra Flying*, finally capitulates to the conditions of real life by giving up his war on money, marrying his pregnant mistress, and going back to work for the New Albion Publicity Company, he is obviously doing something of which his creator approves, and yet critics of the novel frequently cite this ending as its greatest fault. John Wain, claiming that "Orwell originally intended the story to be a sardonic, bitter little parable about what happens to the soul of a society that plants itself in money and still expects to flower," maintains that "in the closing pages everything collapses, tripped up by one of the author's basic confusions. . . . what ought to be a fine, gloomy satiric ending turns unexpectedly into a renascence," and Sir Richard Rees states that "In the end he [Gordon] is a disastrously defeated rebel."

Both of these statements imply that the novel would have been more consistent and that Gordon's conduct would have been more admirable if he had never been blackjacked by Rosemary's pregnancy into reentering middle-class life, if he had been allowed to continue his downward slide into the subworld of poverty. This, in turn, assumes that Gordon was right to declare war on money in the first place, that the moral victory he believed himself to have won by embracing the shabby life of a bookshop assistant was somehow real. Except incidentally, however, is *Keep the Aspidistra Flying* a satire, or even a criticism, of what Gordon calls the "money-world"? The conventional wisdom seems to be that it is. According to the back jacket of my edition, Lionel Trilling regarded it as "a *summa* of all the criticisms of a commercial civilization that have ever been

From *Modern Fiction Studies* 21, no. 1 (Spring 1975). © 1975 by the Purdue Research Foundation.

made," but such a conclusion seems questionable. If Orwell's purpose was to examine a commercial society, he certainly chose an odd perspective. Except in a purely negative way, Gordon is not a creature of the money-world; rather he is a refugee from it. Although he is continually meditating on the horrors concealed behind Corner Table's ratlike smile and the general beastliness of twentieth-century culture, his major preoccupation is not with the evils involved in the possession of money or the desire to possess it but with the evils of being without it. Gordon's rantings against "a civilization of stockbrokers and their lip-sticked wives, of golf, whiskey, ouija-boards and Aberdeen terriers called Jock" ring curiously false, and it is impossible to doubt that he would willingly have traded economic places with his rich parlor-socialist friend Ravelston. Gordon is most convincing when he bewails the bloodiness of life on two quid a week.

To argue that in the course of writing *Keep the Aspidistra Flying* Orwell changed his conception of its meaning, a necessary assumption if we are to believe that the novel begins as an attack on "commercial civilization" and ends as a hymn of praise to middle-class values, is to disregard what he tells us of the roots of Gordon's rebellion. The war on money is born of Gordon's revulsion against the genteel poverty of his spiritless relatives and of his own sense of inferiority:

> Gordon thought it all out, in the naïve selfish manner of a boy. There are two ways to live, he decided. You can be rich, or you can deliberately refuse to be rich. You can possess money, or you can despise money; the one fatal thing is to worship money and fail to get it. He took it for granted that he himself would never be able to make money. It hardly even occurred to him that he might have talents which could be turned to account. That was what his schoolmasters had done for him; they had rubbed into him that he was a seditious little nuisance and not likely to "succeed" in life. He accepted this. Very well, then, he would refuse the whole business of "succeeding"; he would make it his especial purpose *not* to "succeed." Better to reign in hell than serve in heaven; better to serve in hell than serve in heaven, for that matter. Already, at sixteen, he knew which side he was on. He was *against* the money-god and all his swinish priesthood. He had declared war on money; but secretly, of course.

Ten or twelve years ago I saw one of Jules Feiffer's little cartoon stories about a small boy who in the first frame laments, "Eleven years old, and I can't play baseball." In the course of the story, however, he decides that there's "something bad, something unhealthy" about "the way they [the other little boys who can play baseball] *gather* together, the way they *choose* up sides," and by the end he is able to console himself with the reflection that "it's a good thing they wouldn't let me play; otherwise I might never have noticed." This little boy provides an exact analogy to Gordon Comstock, who, because he is convinced that if he makes any attempt to succeed he will only perpetuate the flattened-out, lifeless pattern of the other members of his depressing family, develops a philosophy of dynamic failure. He will make a virtue of necessity. He will not simply slide passively into the inevitable; he will thumb his nose at the success which under any circumstances he believes he can never have and will rush willingly into the arms of poverty.

But Orwell makes it quite clear that this resolve is formed in complete ignorance of the real nature of poverty: "Vaguely he looked forward to some kind of moneyless, anchorite existence. He had a feeling that if you genuinely despise money you can keep going somehow, like the birds of the air. He forgot that the birds of the air don't pay room rent. The poet starving in a garret—but starving, somehow, not uncomfortably—that was his vision of himself."

Along with British imperialism, poverty is one of the major themes of Orwell's early writings, and just as his chief concern with imperialism is the spiritual imprisonment endured by the imperialist, so among the principal horrors of poverty is the crushing burden of isolation it imposes on the poor. The lack of money poisons the relations between men and between men and women, a point driven home again and again by Orwell in his essays and the autobiographical *Down and Out in Paris and London* and by Gordon Comstock in *Keep the Aspidistra Flying*. According to Gordon, most of the inconveniences of living on two quid a week are social: you can't go down to the Crichton for a quick one with Flaxman because you don't have any money; Paul Doring doesn't bother to tell you that he's changed the date of his literary tea party because you're poor and, therefore, can be safely ignored; you can only pay your best friend short and infrequent visits because the difference in your incomes makes real equality nearly impossible; and your girl friend won't sleep with you because you can't afford to marry her if she becomes pregnant and because even privacy costs money in a cold climate. Sometimes even the money you do have doesn't do any good; witness Gordon's Joey:

> Because how can you buy anything with a threepenny-bit? It isn't a coin, it's the answer to a riddle. You look such a fool

when you take it out of your pocket, unless it's in among a
whole handful of other coins. "How much?" you say. "Threepence," the shop-girl says. And then you feel all round your
pocket and fish out that absurd little thing, all by itself, sticking
on the end of your finger like a tiddlywink. The shop-girl sniffs.
She spots immediately that it's your last threepence in the
world. You see her glance quickly at it—she's wondering
whether there's a piece of Christmas pudding still sticking to it.
And you stalk out with your nose in the air, and can't ever go
to that shop again.

With reference to another passage, but one also involving the infa-
mous Joey, David L. Kubal claims that "Orwell satirizes Gordon's vanity
and obsession with money," and certainly there is something a trifle neurotic about Gordon's preoccupation with his own poverty, but it is an error to assume that Orwell is merely poking fun at his harried, moth-eaten
little hero. If Gordon is neurotic, his neurosis is endemic to his condition.

Describing elsewhere his own experience in Paris of having to make
ends meet on six francs (approximately one shilling) a day, Orwell comments that "it was too difficult to leave much thought for anything else,"
and, although his income is five or six times what Orwell's was, the same
holds true for Gordon. Gordon's fixation on his money troubles tends to
make us despise him as a self-pitying little weakling until it is understood
within the context of Orwell's other writings on the subject of poverty,
and then we discover that Gordon is merely reflecting what Orwell himself
had found to be the case. All through the beginning of chapter 6, for instance, Gordon laments the fact that the lack of money makes him repulsive to women, a fancy we are reluctant to credit at first but which Orwell
confirms in *Down and Out in Paris and London:* "For the first time I noticed, too, how the attitude of women varies with a man's clothes. When
a badly dressed man passes them they shudder away from him with a quite
frank movement of disgust, as though he were a dead cat."

Another of Gordon's recurring complaints is that the lack of money
has destroyed his capacity to write:

Of all types of human being, only the artist takes it upon him
to say that he "cannot" work. But it is quite true; there *are*
times when one cannot work. Money again, always money!
Lack of money means discomfort, means squalid worries,
means shortage of tobacco, means ever-present consciousness
of failure—above all it means loneliness. How can you be any-

thing but lonely on two quid a week? And in loneliness no decent book was ever written. It was quite certain that *London Pleasures* would never be the poem he had conceived—it was quite certain, indeed, that it would never even be finished.

A year after the publication of *Keep the Aspidistra Flying*, Orwell returned to the relationship between money and artistic achievement: "You can't settle to anything, you can't command the spirit of *hope* in which anything has got to be created, with that dull evil cloud of unemployment hanging over you."

Gordon even reflects many of Orwell's less justifiable pet prejudices. For instance, Gordon believes that the literary establishment, of which the *Primrose Quarterly* serves as a symbol, is a closed corporation whose response to a grubby little interloper such as himself must inevitably be, "We don't want your bloody poems. We only take poems from chaps we were at Cambridge with. You proletarians keep your distance." Indefensible as this may be, it seems to have been Orwell's real opinion. According to George Woodcock, "At the best of times, Orwell was inclined to a kind of mild paranoia in his relationships with the literary world, which he regarded as a racket run by 'nancy poets' and mutual-back-scratchers from Cambridge."

Granted that Gordon is not a tramp or an unemployed coal miner and that his hardships are correspondingly diluted versions of what Orwell experienced and observed in his various contacts with poverty, but they are none the less real; we are not justified in writing off Gordon's analysis of life on two quid a week as simply the whining of a gutless failure because the isolation and spiritual paralysis of which he complains are real. They are the inevitable products of a meager income.

So this is the final wisdom to which Gordon's rebellion has led him. Poverty is revealed as a kind of spiritual death, a squalid, nasty business that isolates a man from normal human contacts and annihilates his ability to create. If the novel has one major organizing idea, it is not the evils of middle-class values or "The deadening effect of serving the money-god"; throughout, Gordon suffers precisely because he has rejected middle-class values and precisely because he has refused to serve the money-god. As is the case in most of Orwell's early work, the central theme of *Keep the Aspidistra Flying* is poverty. Contrary to our expectations, the parody of 1 Cor. 13 that serves as the book's motto, far from being merely a clever little piece of incidental irony, is a literal truth which it is the purpose of the novel to demonstrate.

Gordon is, of course, perfectly well aware of all this and has been from that first moment of sticky boredom on page one. His education, as it were, has already been completed by the beginning of the novel; there is no particular development, no change, in his character. Rather like Marlowe's Faust in the last act, he has really attained his salvation, even as he damns himself. The various chapters simply examine different facets of the essentially static situation into which Gordon's self-imposed poverty has thrust him; he is the same person throughout, but apparently helpless, unable to free himself. All that is needed is something, some catalyst, that will release him to follow his destiny in marriage and the freedom of service to the aspidistra, and this catalyst is provided by Rosemary's pregnancy. Nonetheless, Gordon's salvation is assured from the first chapter.

The reason it is such a foregone conclusion is that Gordon has grasped the essential fact that in wishing London would be blown to hell by squadron after squadron of bombing planes and in hating Corner Table's mindless grin, he is "merely objectifying his own inner misery." As he explains to Ravelston, the degeneracy of Western Culture is really a side-issue with him:

> "If the whole of England was starving except myself and the people I care about, I wouldn't give a damn. . . . All this talk we make—we're only objectifying our own feelings. It's all dictated by what we've got in our pockets. I go up and down London saying it's a city of the dead, and our civilisation's dying, and I wish war would break out, and God knows what; and all it means is that my wages are two quid a week and I wish they were five."

It really isn't much of a jump from recognizing this to giving up the war on money and rejoining the human race under the shade of the aspidistra.

And Gordon really wants to abandon his rebellion. For instance, he recognizes in marriage "a trap set for you by the money-god," and yet he really wants to fall into that trap:

> Nevertheless he perceived that in a way it is necessary to marry. If marriage is bad, the alternative is worse. For a moment he wished that he were married; he pined for the difficulty of it, the reality, the pain. And marriage must be indissoluble, for better for worse, for richer for poorer, till death do you part. The old Christian ideal—marriage tempered by adultery. Commit adultery if you must, but at any rate have the decency to *call* it adultery. None of that American soulmate slop. Have your fun and then sneak home, juice of the forbidden fruit drip-

ping from your whiskers, and take the consequences. Cut-glass whiskey decanters broken over your head, nagging, burnt meals, children crying, clash and thunder of embattled mothers-in-law. Better that, perhaps, than horrible freedom? You'd know, at least, that it was real life that you were living.

These are obviously the thoughts of a man who in some sense has already made up his mind. Given Gordon's perception of the alternatives with which he is faced, it can be nothing but pure funk that keeps him from abandoning the struggle and going back to work for the New Albion.

Speaking of Saint Francis, Kenneth Clark remarks that "his belief that in order to free the spirit we must shed all our earthly goods is the belief that all great religious teachers have had in common—eastern and western, without exception." Divested of its religious significance, this is precisely the kind of freedom through renunciation that Gordon wishes to achieve, but it is a freedom with which only a saint could be happy, and Gordon is not a saint.

Nor is there any indication in the novel that Gordon is in any sense diminished by not being a saint. In his essay on Gandhi, Orwell remarks that "The essence of being human is that one does not seek perfection, that one *is* sometimes willing to commit sins for the sake of loyalty, that one does not push asceticism to the point where it makes friendly intercourse impossible, and that one is prepared in the end to be defeated and broken up by life, which is the inevitable price of fastening one's love upon other human individuals. No doubt alcohol, tobacco, and so forth are things that a saint must avoid, but sainthood is also a thing that human beings must avoid."

For most of us it would be as easy to live any kind of meaningful life outside the money-world as it would be to live outside the atmosphere of the earth. We have to have our incomes and our families, our dreams of material success and our fear of losing our jobs, because for most of us these things in large measure define what it is to be alive. This is what Gordon's rebellion has taught him, and this is the reason that, for most of *Keep the Aspidistra Flying,* his poverty so utterly poisons his life.

Thus Gordon's reintroduction into middle-class life is inevitable; he could not go on picking at the festering sores of his economic malnutrition forever. Rosemary's pregnancy was, in Aristotelian terms, the efficient cause of his apostasy, but the final cause was his own realization of what is actually entailed in refusing to live within the shadow of the aspidistra.

Once the novel is understood within these terms, the problem of its ending disappears. Gordon's choice was never between the New Albion

Publicity Company and an heroic struggle to escape the deadening influ-
ences of a capitalistic society, but between the New Albion Publicity Company and spiritual death. In the end, he commits a sin for the sake of loyalty, loyalty to Rosemary and their unborn child, and in committing that
sin he recaptures his humanity. Living in the money-world involves a measure of corruption, but at least it is living; the only other alternative involves cutting oneself off from the things that let us know we are alive. In
the end, Gordon makes the inevitable, the only right decision. The price of
purity is simply too high.

JEFFREY MEYERS

Orwell's Apocalypse:
Coming Up for Air

They were born after 1914 and are therefore incapable of happiness.
—BERTRAND RUSSELL

Coming Up for Air (1939), Orwell's central transitional work, is both a synthetic and seminal book, gathering the themes that had been explored in the poverty books of the thirties and anticipating the cultural essays and political satires of the next decade. The location and central symbol of the novel appear as early as *Down and Out* when Orwell describes tramping in Lower Binfield and fishing in the Seine; but the novel has much closer affinities to *Keep the Aspidistra Flying*, for Gordon Comstock's belief that our civilization is dying and the whole world will soon be blown up is very like Bowling's. Similarly, Comstock's fulmination against marriage and his dreadful vision of a million fearful slaves groveling before the throne of money are repeated in the later novel. Comstock's fellow lodger and sometime friend, the traveling salesman Flaxman, has the same good humor, stout physique, and mild vanity of Bowling; and he, too, uses some extra money to escape from his wife.

The dull, shabby, dead-alive Comstock family, who depressingly dwell in an atmosphere of semi-genteel failure, resemble the decayed middle-class family of Hilda Bowling whose vitality has been sapped by poverty. Like the Oxford don Porteous, whose name suggests old wine and Latin, they live "inside the whale," entirely in the dead world of the past. When everything else has changed for the worse, only Hilda's fossilized Anglo-Indian family and the eternally classical Porteous have stayed the same, and their political vacuum has been filled by the hateful Left Book Club lecturer.

From *Modern Fiction Studies* 21, no. 1 (Spring 1975). © 1975 by the Purdue Research Foundation.

"All the decent people are paralysed. Dead men and live gorillas": "The best lack all conviction, while the worst/Are full of passionate intensity."

   The Road to Wigan Pier satirizes many of the same targets as this novel: drab and soulless estate housing, mild and mindless Socialists, the crankish fruit-juice drinker, nudist, and sandal-wearer of Pixy Glen, and the difficulty of finding unpolluted streams with live fish in them. And one of the most striking images of working-class life in *Wigan Pier* is repeated in *Coming Up.* The decrepit woman who had "the usual exhausted face of the slum girl who is twenty-five and looks forty, thanks to miscarriages and drudgery" becomes Bowling's boyhood nursemaid: "A wrinkled-up hag of a woman, with her hair coming down and a smokey face, looking at least fifty years old. . . . It was Katie, who must have been twenty-seven." As in *Wigan Pier,* the deterioration and decay of the natural landscape is paralleled by a similar decline that Bowling observes in people. In the early twenties, Hilda Bowling was a "pretty, delicate girl . . . and within only about three years she's settled down into a depressed, lifeless, middle-aged frump." When he returns to Binfield in the thirties, Elsie, his first love, "with her milky-white skin and red mouth and kind of dull-gold hair, had turned into this great round-shouldered hag, shambling along on twisted heels."

   Finally, Orwell's idealization of domestic life in *Wigan Pier* is repeated in the novel when Bowling's parents read the Sunday newspaper:

> A Sunday afternoon—summer, of course, always summer—a smell of roast pork and greens still floating in the air, and Mother on one side of the fireplace, starting off to read the latest murder but gradually falling asleep with her mouth open, and Father on the other, in slippers and spectacles, working his way slowly through yards of smudgy print . . . and myself under the table with the B.O.P. [Boys' Own Paper], making believe that the tablecloth is a tent.

This Dickensian description of sentimental and soporific, cozy and mindless domestic dullness would be used satirically by most modern writers, but Orwell portrays the scene from the point of view of a secure and protected child.

   Bowling's prophetic fears about the destruction of his childhood England by bombs follow inevitably from Orwell's ambivalent thoughts in the final paragraph of *Homage to Catalonia* as he returns to England:

> Down here it was still the England I had known in my childhood: the railway-cuttings smothered in wild flowers, the deep

meadows where the great shining horses browse and meditate, the slow-moving streams bordered by willows, the green bosoms of the elms, the larkspurs in the cottage gardens ... all sleeping the deep sleep of England, from which I sometimes fear that we shall never wake till we are jerked out of it by the roar of bombs.

Orwell says that "the phrase that Hitler coined for the Germans, 'a sleep-walking people,' would have been better applied to the English," and the somnolence of this pleasant pastoral nostalgia is clearly related to the drowsy numbness of mother and father at the fireplace.

Coming Up for Air is about an apocalyptic vision that destroys a nostalgic dream of childhood. For Bowling is in a prophetic mood in which he foresees the end of the world and can feel things cracking and collapsing under his feet. The war that will decide the destiny of Europe is due in 1941, and it seems to Bowling (as it did to Orwell at the end of *Homage*) that he "could see the whole of England, and all the people in it, and all the things that will happen to all of them." Bowling, caught in a brief intense moment between the destructive future and the nostalgic past, seeks, like Winston Smith, to escape the painful modern realities by recapturing his idealized childhood memories. Orwell's metaphor of escape in both works (people trapped in a sinking ship is the symbol of man's fate in *1984*) is "coming up for air," "like the big sea-turtles when they come paddling up to the surface, stick their noses out and fill their lungs with a great gulp before they sink down again among the seaweed and octopuses." But escape is impossible for Bowling, who has the archetypal experience of returning home to discover that the lost Eden of childhood is irrecoverable:

> What's the good of trying to revisit the scenes of your boyhood? They don't exist. Coming up for air! But there isn't any air. The dustbin we're in reaches up to the stratosphere.

The childhood passages of *Coming Up* have the same affectionate and nostalgic tone as Orwell's "As I Please" column and his major essays on English popular culture, like "Boys' Weeklies." These essays, which develop and illuminate the themes of the novel, were written against the background of the Second World War. In one of these cultural essays, "The Art of Donald McGill" (1941), Orwell lists the conventions of the comic postcard jokes—all women plot marriage, which only benefits women; all husbands are henpecked; middle-aged men are drunkards; nudism is comical; Air Raid precautions are ludicrous; illegitimate babies and old maids are always funny—and nearly every one of them appears in

Coming Up. Actually, Bowling's colloquial humor is far superior to these conventional jokes. He "baptises" his new false teeth in a pub, compares Hilda's constriction to that of an "average zenana," says that one old lady thought the Left Book Club had to do with books left in railway carriages, and observes that he got fat "so suddenly that it was as if a cannon ball had hit me and got stuck inside." Orwell's description of Bowling guarding the tins of bully-beef in Cornwall, and especially his satire on Hilda's (and his own) Anglo-Indian family and on Porteous, both mummified relics of the past, is well done. *Coming Up*, like *Gem* and *Magnet*, *Raffles* (all three are mentioned in the novel), comic postcards, *Helen's Babies*, Bertie Wooster and Jeeves, and "Good Bad Books," recreates a decent, stable, familiar but nonexistent world.

In each of his essays on popular culture, Orwell favorably compares the static old-fashioned view expressed in these works with that of their harsher and crueler successors: the schoolboy atmosphere of *Raffles* and "Boys' Weeklies" with the torture and corruption of *No Orchids for Miss Blandish* and the "Yank mags," the classic perfect poison murder with the modern bloody "Cleft Chin Murder." (The closing paragraphs of "Raffles" and "Decline" are nearly identical.) All these popular works are Orwell's boyhood favorites, have a strictly pre-War outlook, and never mention contemporary politics. Popular books like *Helen's Babies* and *Little Women* "have something that is perhaps best described as integrity, or good morale." Their world, like that of Lower Binfield at the turn of the century, was more class-ridden and more impoverished than the modern world, but did not have an oppressive sense of helplessness. As Orwell says in an unpublished BBC talk,

> What you are not likely to find in the mind of anyone in the year 1900, is a doubt about the continuity of civilisation. If the world as people saw it then was rather harsh, simple and slow-moving, it was also secure. Things would continue in a more or less recognisable pattern; life might not get appreciably more pleasant, but at any rate barbarism wouldn't return.

This opposition between past and present is symbolized by the house in Binfield that is cleaved by the accidental bomb: "What was extraordinary was that in the upstairs rooms nothing had been touched . . . but the lower rooms had caught the force of the explosion. There was a frightful smashed-up mess." Both the pre-War past and the warlike present have rather obvious contrasting characteristics. In old Lower Binfield there was no rush and no fear, in West Bletchley everyone is "scared stiff"; in the past the airplane was "a flimsy, rickety-looking thing," in the present threatening bombers constantly fly overhead; in the pre-War world fish swim in the pond, in the modern world, writes John Wain, "fish is the stuff they put into sausages instead of meat":

> Ersatz, they call it. I remembered reading that *they* were making sausages out of fish, and fish, no doubt, out of something differ-ent. It gave me the feeling that I'd bitten into the modern world and discovered what it was really made of. . . . But when you come down to brass tacks and get your [false] teeth into some-thing solid, a sausage for instance, that's what you get. Rotten fish in a rubber skin. Bombs of filth bursting inside your mouth.

The explosive and perverse phallic image emphasizes the corruption and sterility of Lower Binfield. Orwell frequently protests against "the in-stinctive horror which all sensitive people feel at the progressive mechani-zation of life"; and in one of his rare poems, "On a Ruined Farm near the His Master's Voice Gramophone Factory," he grieves that "The acid smoke has soured the fields, / And browned the few and windworn flow-ers." These lines echo the tradition that goes back to Blake and that has been voiced most powerfully in the modern age by Lawrence (in *Lady Chatterley's Lover*) and by Forster, whose views in *Abinger Pageant* (1934) are similar to Orwell's:

> Houses and bungalows, hotels, restaurants and flats, arterial roads, by-passes, petrol pumps and pylons—are these going to be England? Are these man's final triumph? Or is there another England, green and eternal, which will outlast them?

Orwell's symbol of England's green and pleasant land is fishing, "the opposite of war," and so much of the novel is concerned with fishing that Orwell might have subtitled his book, which takes place near Walton, *The Compleat Angler*. Yet it remains an effective symbol:

> The very idea of sitting all day under a willow tree beside a quiet pool—and being able to find a quiet pool to sit beside— belongs to the time before the war. . . . There's a kind of peace-fulness even in the names of English coarse fish. . . . They're solid kinds of names.

The ideal fishing pool is the secret one behind Binfield House where enor-mous carp perhaps a hundred years-old sun themselves near the tranquil surface of the water. When Bowling finally returns there, he finds the Thames crowded and polluted and the sacred pool a drained cavern half full of tin cans.

Isaac Rosenfeld's shrewd observation that Orwell "was a radical in politics and a conservative in feeling," both a socialist and a man in love with the past, explains why Orwell is so deeply ambivalent about the pre-War period. He criticizes the English for "obstinately clinging to everything that is out of date and a nuisance," but creates an ideal pub, "The Moon under Water," in which "everything has the solid comfortable ugliness of the nineteenth century." He praises the postcards of Donald McGill, for "there is no sign in them of any attempt to induce an outlook acceptable to the ruling class," but he calls "Boys' Weeklies" "sodden in the worst illusions of 1910" because they inculcate pernicious social and political attitudes: the boys "get what they are looking for, but they get it wrapped up in the illusions which their future employers think suitable for them." In "England Your England," he states that both the common people and the intellectuals must and do oppose the existing social order, yet he also attacks the pre-War world of "Boys' Weeklies" that is very similar in mood to his description of Lower Binfield:

> The year is 1910. . . . There is a cosy fire in the study, and outside the wind is whistling. The ivy clusters thickly round the old grey stones. The King is on his throne and the pound is worth a pound. . . . Everything is safe, solid and unquestionable. Everything will be the same for ever and ever.

Since Orwell believes "one of the dominant facts in English life during the past three-quarters of a century has been the decay of ability in the ruling class" and since all the peace and serenity of pre-War England depends on the leisure of the few and the labor of the many, he admires the working, lower-middle, and middle-class aspects of the pre-War world but attacks the upper-middle and upper-class characteristics. In "Such, Such Were the Joys," Orwell both criticizes and cherishes the decent but rather decadent "age of *The Merry Widow,* Saki's novels and *Peter Pan*" and describes the

> atmosphere, as it were, of eating everlasting strawberry ices on green lawns to the tune of the Eton Boating Song. The extraordinary thing was the way in which everyone took it for granted that this oozing, bulging wealth of the English upper and upper-middle classes would last forever, and was part of the order of things. After 1918 it was never quite the same again.

And in *Coming Up,* *Pixy* Glen, like *Wendy's* Tea Shoppe, represents a spurious attempt by the lower-middle classes to climb upwards by returning to the artificiality of Barrie's pre-War world.

"I am not able, and I do not *want,* completely to abandon the world-view that I acquired in childhood," writes Orwell; and when in the summer of 1940 he escaped into the country with his dog "Marx" and had two glorious days at Wallington, in Hertfordshire village "the whole thing took me straight back to my childhood, perhaps the last bit of that kind of life that I shall ever have." Though Orwell yearns to return to his boyhood years, it is rather difficult to reconcile his childhood nostalgia with the grim tortures of "Such, Such Were the Joys." It would seem that this ideal childhood existed only in Orwell's imagination and that his works represent a fairly consistent attempt to recreate and perpetuate this myth.

Orwell has a keen desire to establish a continuity between the England of the past and the present and is particularly attracted to writers who, like T. S. Eliot, carry on the human heritage by "keeping in touch with pre-war emotions." The most perfect embodiment of the pre-War myth of eternal ease and blue summer skies is Brooke's "The Old Vicarage, Grantchester" (1912), and in "The Captain's Doll," Lawrence also writes with retrospective nostalgia about these peaceful years which "seemed lovely, almost like before the war: almost the same feeling of eternal holiday, as if the world was made for man's everlasting holiday." Reviewing Edmund Blunden's *Cricket Country,* Orwell states "the essential thing in this book, as in nearly everything that Mr. Blunden writes, is his nostalgia for the golden age before 1914, when the world was peaceful as it has never since been"; and he says almost the same thing about H. G. Wells, whose greatest gift "was his power to convey the atmosphere of the golden years between 1890 and 1914." Wells's *The History of Mr. Polly* (1910) has a strong effect on Bowling, and, as Orwell says of *Coming Up* in a letter to Julian Symons, "Of course the book was bound to suggest Wells watered down. I have a great admiration for Wells as a writer, and he was a very early influence on me."

This golden tranquillity was shattered forever by the kind of modern war that Bowling experienced in Flanders and Orwell fought in Spain. The unrefrigerated backyard of the Binfield butcher "smelt like a battlefield"; the ravaged landscape of "tincans, turds, mud, weeds, clumps of rusty barbed wire" is exactly like the catalogue of the Aragon front; both Orwell and Bowling try to escape war by fishing; and the description of Bowling's explosive wound derives from that day at Huesca when Orwell was shot through the throat. Bowling believes that if war did not kill you it was bound to make you think about the kind of world that would emerge from the ruins, and some aspects of the world of *1984* already exist in *Coming Up:* the blunt razor-blades, the nasty gusts of wind, the vision of the seedy smashed streets. Bowling finds a severed leg at a bomb site just as Winston Smith finds a severed hand; and, like Winston, the cringing victims in the housing estate lick the hand that wallops them. The red-armed and fertile-bellied prole washerwoman is foreshadowed by Bowling's peaceful glimpse of the roofs where the women hang out the washing, and the "Two Minutes of Hate" is anticipated by the enraged *anti*-Fascist (a nice touch) lecturer at the Left Book Club. Bowling fears the postwar totalitarian State even more than the cataclysmic war, and the Oceania of *1984* is foreshadowed in *Coming Up:*

> *It's all going to happen.* All the things you've got at the back of your mind, the things you're terrified of, the things you tell yourself are just a nightmare or only happen in foreign countries. The bombs, the food-queues, the rubber truncheons, the barbed wire, the coloured shirts, the slogans, the enormous faces, the machine-guns squirting out of bedroom windows.

Orwell's apocalyptic belief is similar to Henry Miller's, who told Orwell that "Our civilization was destined to be swept away and replaced by something so different that we should scarcely regard it as human. . . . Everywhere there is a sense of the approaching cataclysm." Miller made a powerful impression on Orwell, and his astonishing indifference and passivity about the impending doom was both fascinating and deeply attractive. Miller, perhaps more than any other modern writer, totally rejects Orwell's concept of decency, his vague but important term for the synthesis of the traditional English virtues that he describes in "England Your England": gentleness, fairness, integrity, unselfishness, comradeship, patriotism, respect for legality, belief in justice, liberty, and truth. In the world of modern power politics, especially as Orwell describes it, these qualities barely survive: they exist in Wiltshire perhaps, but not in Whitehall. One of his major weaknesses is that he puts too much faith in this ineffectual and disappearing decency, for decent men seldom achieve political power, and if they do, they rarely remain decent. Yet Orwell feels the need to believe in *something*—"The real problem is how to restore the religious attitude while accepting death as final"—and there is nothing else left to believe in *but* decency.

Miller's extreme immorality and sensuality and his imaginative intensity are precisely the qualities that Orwell lacks, and his social radicalism is characteristically American just as Orwell's conservatism is typically English. Orwell's profound and ambiguous attraction (revealed in his long essay and three enthusiastic book reviews on Miller) to someone who could remain so oblivious and insulated, illuminates Orwell's strange ambivalence about preserving the past and about his intense commitment to the concept of decency.

Like Miller, James Joyce also rejects decency and remains supremely indifferent to modern politics. As Orwell says, Joyce wrote "*Ulysses* in Switzerland, with an Austrian passport and a British pension, during the 1914–18 war, to which he paid as nearly as possible no attention." Orwell is extremely enthusiastic about *Ulysses,* studies it carefully, and writes about it frequently. In a letter of 1933 he states, "Joyce interests me so much that I can't stop talking about him once I start"; and the following year he makes a witty comparison between himself and the author of *Ulysses* in a Joycean sexual-musical image:

> When I read a book like that and then come back to my own work, I feel like a eunuch who has taken a course in voice production and can pass himself off fairly well as a bass or baritone, but if you listen closely you can hear the good old squeak just the same as ever.

Orwell's novel has several Joycean echoes. The firm of Wilson & Bloom builds houses on Bowling's street; Orwell's epigraph, "He's dead, but he won't lie down" recalls the song "Finnegan's Wake"; and Bowling reads Molly's favorite author, Paul de Kock.

Orwell's many statements about *Ulysses* illuminate the central theme of his own novel—the lost world of childhood and the fearful despair of ordinary people in the modern world—as well as the personality and character of Bowling, who is modeled on Leopold Bloom:

> Here is a whole world of stuff which you have lived with since childhood, stuff which you supposed to be of its nature incommunicable and somebody has managed to communicate it. The effect is to break down, at any rate momentarily, the solitude in which the human being lives. When you read certain passages in *Ulysses* you feel that Joyce's mind and your mind are one, that he knows all about you though he has never heard your name, that there exists some world outside time and space in which you and he are together. And though he does not re-

semble Joyce in other ways, there is a touch of this quality in Henry Miller.

[*Ulysses*] sums up better than any book I know the fearful despair that is almost normal in modern times.

Books about ordinary people behaving in an ordinary manner are extremely rare, because they can only be written by someone who is capable of standing both inside and outside the ordinary man, as Joyce for instance stands inside and outside Bloom.

[Bloom has] a streak of intellectual curiosity.... [He] is a rather exceptionally sensitive specimen of the man in the street, and I think the especial interest of this is that the cultivated man and the man in the street so rarely meet in modern literature.

While writing *Coming Up*, Orwell describes Bowling as being, like Bloom, "rather thoughtful and fairly well-educated, even slightly bookish." Though Bloom and Bowling (their names are similar though Bowling suggests the bourgeois bowler hat) are not comparable in depth of characterization (the bass and the eunuch), and Bowling is more brash and hardened, they both are intelligent, curious, perceptive, sympathetic, good natured, humorous, and vulgar, and both are nostalgic about a happier past. Both characters are "ordinary middling chaps," and both are salesmen, though Bowling is more successful and feels superior to the two newspaper canvassers (Bloom's job) whom he meets on the train to London. Both know many obscure "scientific" facts; Bowling's mind, like Bloom's, "goes in jerks"; and the thought of the Albanian King Zog "starts memories" of King Og of Bashan and transports Bowling back to his "incommunicable" childhood through a Joycean "stream of consciousness" that attempts to capture the past:

The past is a curious thing. It's with you all the time. I suppose an hour never passes without your thinking of things that happened ten or twenty years ago.... Then some chance sight or sound or smell, especially smell, sets you going, and the past doesn't merely come back to you, you're actually *in* the past.

In 1948 Orwell responded to Julian Symons's criticism of *Coming Up* and said: "Of course you are perfectly right about my own character constantly intruding on that of the narrator. I am not a real novelist anyway, and that particular vice is inherent in writing a novel in the first person, which one should never do." This frank admission of his lack of imaginative power (and his need to write for money) explains why Orwell's books have so much in common and why his novels are so often nourished by his essays. It also explains his eager receptivity to the influence of Joyce and of D. H. Lawrence, to whom he also alludes in his novel.

A man named Mellors gives Bowling the racing tip that provides his escape money; and like Lawrence's Mellors, Bowling rises to the officer class during the War and becomes, temporarily, a gentleman. Lawrence's story "The Thorn in the Flesh" is referred to in the novel, and Bowling enjoys reading *Sons and Lovers*. More significantly, the mood of *Coming Up*, and, indeed, of many of Orwell's works of the thirties, is close to the opening sentences of *Lady Chatterley's Lover*—"Ours is essentially a tragic age, so we refuse to take it tragically. The cataclysm has happened, we are among the ruins"—and to the dark prophecies of Lawrence's letters:

> I am so sad, for my country, for this great wave of civilisation, 2000 years, which is now collapsing, that it is hard to live. So much beauty and pathos of old things passing away and no new things coming . . . the winter stretches ahead, where all vision is lost and all memory dies out.

A disintegrating civilization on the verge of an annihilating war has been the subject of the greatest novels of our time—*Women in Love*, *Remembrance of Things Past*, *The Magic Mountain*—and *Coming Up* belongs *thematically* with these books. Written a generation later, the novel conveys many of the modes of thought and feeling characteristic of Orwell's age—the uncertainty, fear, and despair that is expressed in Spengler's *Decline of the West* and Yeats's "The Second Coming," in Miller's *Tropic of Cancer* and Auden's "September 1, 1939." As Leonard Woolf writes in his autobiography:

> In 1914 in the background of one's life and one's mind there were light and hope; by 1918 one had unconsciously accepted a perpetual public menace and darkness and had admitted in the privacy of one's mind or soul an iron fatalistic acquiescence in insecurity and barbarism.

While working on *Coming Up*, Orwell writes to Cyril Connolly in Gadarene imagery: "Everything one writes now is overshadowed by this ghastly feeling that we are rushing towards a precipice and, though we shan't actually prevent ourselves or anyone else from going over, must put up some sort of fight." Despite the grim prognostications, Bowling opposes the threatening cataclysm. His imaginative preservation of the past is the positive core in the novel that survives the present horrors and ultimately conveys the most powerful effect in the book. As Bowling says, "I'm fat but I'm thin inside. Has it ever struck you that there's a thin man [the past] inside every fat man [the present]?" and this preservation of the past in the free minds of helpless yet resisting men was one of Orwell's central concerns in both *Animal Farm* and *1984*.

CLEO McNELLY KEARNS

On Not Teaching Orwell

If recent articles in *Newsweek* and the *Chronicle of Higher Education* are any guide, we are in the midst of yet another crisis in the schools, this time in the teaching of language skills. Students, it seems, can neither read nor write, and there is something of a panic on as a result. One cause of this crisis lies in the entrance of new kinds of students into the university: working-class, minority, and even middle-class students whose training has simply not prepared them for written communication. Clearly, something is needed here, and equally clearly the solution has not yet been found. Although many approaches and materials are on trial, from old-fashioned or "bonehead" English as one source calls it, to methods based on new theories of rhetoric, psychology, and stylistics, so far none of these has proved its worth for long enough to dominate the field.

In a situation like this one where we are not sure what does work, it may be useful to consider what does not. Negative criticism has its place, as writers like Edward Said and Fredric Jameson are helping us to see, and at times there are enough practical as well as theoretical considerations at stake to force the issue. In this case, the target is an especially relevant one—the work of George Orwell—whose essays are prime examples, in my opinion, of how *not* to teach composition. Many other teachers share this view, for reasons it is important to make clear.

The point might be moot if textbooks did not keep on pouring off the press promising all things to all English teachers and offering over and over the same set of Orwell essays: "Politics and the English Language,"

From *College English* 38, no. 6 (February 1977). © 1977 by the National Council of Teachers of English.

"A Hanging," "Shooting an Elephant," and "Marrakech." At the same time, curiously enough, Orwell is rarely taught at the advanced, not to mention the graduate, levels. It is as if we do not want to admit this disturbing writer "above stairs," however salutary we think he may be for freshmen in composition. The reasons for this ambivalence are complex and important for criticism and pedagogy as well.

Students, for instance, especially at what some teachers call the remedial or beginning level, do not find Orwell helpful at all. Most of them, in my classes at least, tend to respond to his prose with a neutral or negative stare. When they are pushed to formulate this response they do so with a unanimity that is often hard to understand. Orwell is "dull," "cold," and "boring"; or, on a more sophisticated level, he is "impersonal," "difficult," "biased," and even "unclear." These are certainly not terms that I would apply to that lucid, graceful style. Many of them, of course, reflect either standard resistance to new material or real reading problems—inability to hear irony, for example. After some time and study, however, I have begun to understand that there are deeper problems at work with Orwell than these, and that student descriptions refer to *something*, even when they are not sure quite to what. The resistance here is of a different order and kind than most, and it takes some critical evaluation to find out why.

Mina Shaughnessy, in a paper given at Livingston College in the fall of 1975, offers a starting point. First, she urges teachers never to overlook a student's own analysis of writing and reading blocks, even when this sounds simple or naïve. For instance, she points out, students often mention limited vocabulary as a cause of their deficiency in writing skills. This analysis is not always so wide of the mark: grammatical problems often mask lexical ones, and the traditional teacherly prejudice against the thesaurus may be a mistake. Then, too, when they criticize writing models as "too difficult," even when these have been chosen for clarity and concreteness of reference, beginning readers are often reflecting the real complexity of an apparently casual style. Orwell's own writing is an example of this complexity, Shaughnessy says. Furthermore, in direct contradiction to Orwell and others, Shaughnessy stresses the importance of clichés and bureaucratic formulae in the development of writing ability. These are often, to the inexperienced writer, important ways of moving in to the reading / writing role, and here as elsewhere, to borrow the formulation of Basil Bernstein, *if you can't manage the role, you can't produce the appropriate speech.*

In light of Shaughnessy's paper, the negative dynamic between Orwell's writing and student response begins to make a little more sense. That dynamic is, moreover, complicated by Orwell's own assumptions about language and by the nature of his audience in a present-day writing class. There are at least two different levels on which Orwell doesn't "work" here: the level of style, where his advice is not only misdirected but fails to account for his own success as a writer; and the level of content, where his narrative stance and the attitudes and values it implies directly contravene the experience of the students we most need to reach. In discussing the first level, that of style, I will be relying most heavily on "Politics and the English Language" and Orwell's autobiographical writings read in the light of the work of Basil Bernstein and William Labov in linguistics, and of the critical work of Raymond Williams, Terry Eagleton, and Alex Zwerdling. On the second level, that of content, I want to look at the important essay "Marrakech." In both cases the readings have been informed by and are related to student work.

One of Shaughnessy's major points, as I have said, is her stress on the use of cliché, bureaucratic or formulaic language, and even at times the imitation of "jargon" as a means of working in to the writer/reader role. All of these devices can be ways of interweaving personal experience of the world through one's own "native" language with public discourse, which is at the same time more formal and more bound by convention than private speech. In these terms, the use of a threadbare device that makes the average English teacher wince can in fact be a provisional gain for the student, and almost certainly comes at the cost of some effort on his or her part.

All of these points are in fact explicitly contradicted in Orwell's "Politics and the English Language," which makes the classic argument for an original and personal prose style. Of course, the major problem is that Orwell presumes his readers have already been taught to write—badly. This presumption may be true of the average academic, but it is certainly not true of the students we see in our classes today. Their problem is that they have hardly been taught to write at all, which gives them both advantages and disadvantages.

From this position, however, they are likely to be seriously misled by Orwell's advice. In "Politics and the English Language," for instance, his dire warnings on the use of cliché and jargon do not even cover his own writing, which is in some ways a highly sophisticated tour de force predicated on the ability to employ them both. Compare, for example, the opening of this essay with that of a beginner's paper from a class at Columbia University's School of General Studies in the spring of 1976:

> Most people who bother with the matter at all would admit
> that the English language is in a bad way, but it is generally

assumed that we cannot by conscious action do anything about it. Our civilization is decadent and our language—so the argument runs—must inevitably share in the general collapse.

"Politics and the English Language"

To Americans food shortage takes place only in other countries. Such countries as Chad, Bangladesh, or even some South American countries have food shortages but not in the United States. In this paper I will attempt to make the reader aware of the food shortages today.

"Food Crisis"

In terms of their rhetorical strategy, the intent of these passages is the same: to raise and call into question a widely held assumption about the world. Orwell, however, clearly possesses a greater range of techniques for doing this than the student. There is the control of tone, somewhat self-deprecating in the opening notes, but rising almost to parody in the second sentence. There is the manipulation of levels of discourse, marked by the dash, to distinguish the narrator's point of view from the argument summarized. There is the somewhat disingenous "we" which glosses over the distinctions so clearly set up at first between the writer and "most people," and which by doing so dramatizes the error under discussion, that of letting language slide into decay by lack of precision and care. Furthermore, on the level of diction alone, this opening demonstrates Orwell's ability to move, when necessary, from the mocking, journalistic cliché of "in a bad way" to the editorializing jargon of "decadent." Neither of these word choices is innocent. Orwell does not use "in a bad way" only because it approximates spoken language but also because it is vague and over-general and because it mimics an attitude he wishes to explode. Likewise "decadent" not only refers to a certain theory, but caricatures those who would use the word that way, with just that tone of passive relish. Orwell's style here is less a "windowpane," as he likes to call it, than a special-angle lens.

The student is, of course, nowhere near Orwell's mastery of those techniques. He writes too cryptically, too much inside his own head, leaving out crucial markers of level, shifters, and even a requisite subject and verb. To move fully into the written code he needs, for instance, to be able to add the rather strange formula "is something that" to the first sentences and to make explicit its implicit connection with the third. He also needs some way to refine on the rhetorical force of "*even* some South American countries" (emphasis added), though this in itself is a remarkable step forward, in that it sketches out an attitude he wants to criticize and to separate off from his own train of thought. Most of all this student needs to be able to "see" the inherent comedy of syntax which leaves Chad judiciously refraining from creating its food shortage in the middle of the U.S.A. (I have always found this kind of mistake extremely difficult to explain to students, partly, I think because it stems from the gulf between written and spoken language. In speech, where context "counts" for more, the meaning would be clear and the sentence would pass without comment. In writing, context has less power, at least over syntax, and the code requires a high degree of articulation to work.)

The last sentence, with its shopworn "in this paper I will attempt" is, of course, debatable. I would argue, following Shaughnessy, that the formula is important here and represents a provisional gain in that it keeps the reader in the picture and provides a steadying sense of role. I think the normal teacher response is actually less of a wince than a sigh of relief—this writer has at least got back a measure of control. At some point he may be able to do so in a less conventional way.

At almost all of these points, however, Orwell will fail him as a guide, if not as a model as well. Simply look at the rules he propounds:

1. *Never use a metaphor, simile or other figure of speech which you are used to seeing in print.* (But this student is not used to identifying *any* metaphors or similes in print. It would be nice if he were, and if he ventured one or two or even the more common ones in this paper. Orwell's fear of cliché here is not only beside the point, but fails to take account of the complexity of the process by which metaphors move from "live" to "dead" in the language, and can be familiar or unfamiliar in different ways as a result.)

2. *Never use a long word where a short one will do.* (Again, this advice presumes an active lexicon of word choices, which the student doesn't have, and which he can only get by practice in moving from synonym to synonym both up and down the ladder of abstraction. The substitution of a few latinate words for Anglo-Saxon ones will help, not hurt, this process and develop reading skills as well.)

3. *If it is possible to cut a word out, always cut it out.* (But the problem for this writer is clearly expansion, not contraction,

another place where students are often correct, if naïve, in their own diagnosis of their inability to "write long enough.")

4. *Never use the passive where you can use the active.* (Perfectly good advice, excellent for all writers. Orwell gets one out of five for this answer.)

5. *Break any of these rules sooner than say anything outright barbarous.* (This is charming and clever. Unfortunately, the acquisition of middle-class and written codes of language is often a matter of some importance in the lives of the students we teach, as it bears directly on their ability to survive. They are understandably nervous about it, and well aware of the social consequences of saying anything "outright barbarous." Their problem is that they do not know what sounds "outright barbarous" especially to middle-class, well-educated ears. Orwell's easy flippancy here can only offend in tone, while returning us to square one in content, since again it does not teach but simply presumes the code.)

The difficulty with Orwell, however, does not lie only in a mistaken set of rules. Involved in his work are presuppositions about language, class and race which both determine his style and severely limit his usefulness in a composition class. Many of these have been discussed brilliantly in terms of literary criticism, as a glance through Raymond Williams's collection of essays on Orwell will show. Alex Zwerdling's *Orwell and the Left* also contains much useful analysis, especially in his chapter on class and audience. Zwerdling makes the point, for instance, that Orwell never considered himself a proletarian writer at all. He knew that the class whose interests he had chosen to defend did not ordinarily read his work, and he chose for the most part to accept this limitation. Only on rare occasions and under the pressure of major events did he attempt to communicate directly with the majority of people on whose behalf he tried to speak.

This stance, whether for good or ill, stems in part from Orwell's enormous sense of the barrier between classes, a barrier in which language plays a crucial role. On this subject Orwell is often eloquent, as this passage from *The Road to Wigan Pier* makes clear:

For some months I lived entirely in coal-miners' houses. I ate my meals with the family, I washed at the kitchen sink, I shared bedrooms with miners, drank beer with them, played darts with them, talked to them by the hour together. But though I was among them, and I hope and trust they did not find me a nuisance, I was not one of them, and they knew it even better than I did. However much you like them, however interesting you find their conversation, there is always the accursed itch of class-difference, like the pea under the princess's mattress. It is not a question of dislike or distaste, only of difference, but it is enough to make real intimacy impossible. Even with miners who described themselves as Communists, I found that it needed tactful manoeuverings to prevent them from calling me "sir"; and all of them, except in moments of great animation, softened their northern accents for my benefit. I liked them and hoped they liked me; but I went among them as a foreigner, and both of us were aware of it. Whichever way you turn this curse of the class-difference confronts you like a wall of stone. Or rather it is not so much like a stone wall as the plate-glass pane of an aquarium; it is so easy to pretend that it isn't there, and so impossible to get through it.

This is Orwell at his best, both as a person and as a writer. He has a special genius, as here, for naming a problem which is usually repressed from genteel or middle-class conversation. His image of the plate-glass in an aquarium not only captures the invisible solidity of class-difference, even in America, but also, in its careful ambiguity about who is inside and who outside, perfectly expresses his own sense of uneasy position. It also, not incidentally, casts an ironic light on his later characterization of good prose as "crystalline" or "like a window-pane." For students, coming from a different class to Orwell's prose, reading his work may be rather like pressing themselves against this invisible glass barrier: "it is so easy to pretend that it isn't there, and so impossible to get through it."

Unfortunately, in many of his essays, Orwell does not sustain this level of consciousness, especially where problems of language and race are concerned. In the passage above it is clear that while the men "talk a different language" than the narrator, that language *exists*, and it exists in a context involving fairly elaborate social and linguistic codes. Beer drinking, dart playing, even washing up and eating are forms of communication with their own rules and meanings, so much is evident. Elsewhere in Orwell, however, this clarity slips away. In "Marrakech," for example, Algerian mourners in the opening section barely seem to bury their dead, simply dumping them into the ground and leaving "no gravestone, no name, no identifying mark of any kind." The implication here is that these people are so poor that they have no customs at all; they simply swarm about, like flies over a corpse. Likewise, they have no language, or if they do, it is only in the most "primitive," oral form. An old woman to whom Orwell gives money (without, I might add, considering what the gesture might mean in her context, where exchanges of any sort between white men and black women are likely to be equivocal indeed) responds only with "a shrill wail, almost a scream, which was partly gratitude but mostly surprise." The passive victim in "A Hanging" speaks only once, and that is to shout "Ram, Ram, Ram, Ram" in a strained, unnatural voice as his dying prayer.

Oddly enough, these images of the oppressed as inarticulate or mute seem to seep back into Orwell's picture of the English working class as well. His description of a typical worker's evening is a case in point: "Father, in his shirtsleeves, sits in the rocking chair at one side of the fire reading the racing finals and Mother sits on the other with her sewing, and the children are happy with a pennorth of mint humbugs." The rest, presumably, is silence. At times, that silence seems to Orwell adequate, even preferable, to middle-class rhetoric; hence his emotion at the simple handshake of the Italian infantryman in *Homage to Catalonia*. But it is often true that his class and race-bound sense of what constitutes effective discourse prevents him from "hearing" other codes and leads him to believe that working people have a fragmented, inarticulate or "oral" form of speech.

A valuable counter to this view may be found in the recent work of Basil Bernstein and William Labov in linguistics, and some of their formulations bear directly on Orwell's prose style as well. In particular, Bernstein's comparative study of sociolinguistic codes among middle- and working-class people is significant. He argues that these classes not only use different language codes but use them in a different way. He describes the middle-class code as "expanded," that is making its linguistic principles and operations explicit and creating its own metalanguages of criticism, power and control. Working-class speech on the other hand tends to be "context bound," having its base in condensed symbols that can be understood only with reference to a specific situation. In middle-class speech, says Bernstein, "the 'I' stands over the 'We' " and "meanings which are discreet to the speaker must be offered so that they are intelligible to the listener." These values necessitate a highly explicit code. In working-class speech, there is likely to be a strong metaphoric element, and "the speaker may be more concerned with how something is said and when it is said, and silence takes on a variety of meanings." Working-class speech is based on *consensus* and *community,* middle-class speech on *differentiation* and *individual roles.*

There are some problems with Bernstein's formulation, not least of which that it tends to impute rational thinking and intellectual power only to the middle class. (Labov's well-known essay "The Logic of Non-Standard English" is an important corrective to this view.) But if Bernstein's formulations are questionable on the level of speech, they seem to me remarkably useful when it comes to the difference between a beginner's writing and that of a person trained to use the middle-class code. There could, after all, be no more accurate description of Orwell's narrative stance than that the " 'I' stands over the 'We' "; and "context-bound" perfectly captures a certain quality of much initial student work, which often contains no concessions to the need to be explicit at all. For the really beginning student, writing is often bounded strictly by the act of putting down words on paper, with no sense of the wider context of "being read." In academic writing, the middle-class code as here described is not only conventional but effective and necessary, because it demands explication and expansion at all times. Both codes, however, have their roots in social patterns ultimately related to class.

Orwell, of course, had no access to these ideas, and his theories of language remain determined on the one hand by his partial deafness to working-class speech and on the other by his own ambivalence about his social place. "Propaganda and Demotic Speech" for example, an essay written under the pressure of World War II, is almost entirely guided by the notion of rustic oral simplicity in the masses. "The first step" in addressing the working class, Orwell says, "is to find out which of the abstract words habitually used by politicians are really understood by large numbers of people. Secondly, in writing one can keep the spoken word constantly in mind. . . . Say to yourself, 'Could I simplify this? Could I make it more like speech?' " "Politics and the English Language" though more thoughtful, is based, as we have seen, on many of the same assumptions.

The problem here is that a movement in the direction of speech in writing will not necessarily result in prose that is clearer to the great majority of people. The double distance between working-class speech and middle-class writing, a distance made up not only of the gap between all written and all spoken language but of that between the two codes as well, cannot be bridged in this way. Actually, what Orwell often seems to want is to return language, and political language in particular, to the private sector. He says:

> In our time it is broadly true that political writing is bad writing. When it is not true, it will generally be found that the writer is some kind of rebel, expressing his private opinions, not a "party line."

One almost never finds in political prose, he says, "a fresh, vivid, homemade turn of speech." This observation is immediately followed, curiously enough, by a repetition of the oldest and most mechanical stereotype of the communist, a stereotype Orwell produces as automatically as any political hack. With this kind of speaker, Orwell says,

> one often has a curious feeling that one is not watching a live human being but some kind of dummy: a feeling which suddenly becomes stronger at moments when the light catches the speaker's spectacles and turns them into blank discs which seem to have no eyes behind them.

Even for Orwell, apparently, a cliché of political rhetoric has its use.

All of Orwell's theories of language and writing, however, can themselves be "decoded" for their meaning in terms of social class. His advice on avoiding abstractions and his careful attempts to approximate common speech, for instance, are both movements away from the "purple prose" that attracted him when he was young. This stage in his life was bound up with feelings of inferiority that came, in part at least, from his position as a lower-middle-class student in a solidly middle-class school. In "Why I Write" he says, "I think from the very start my literary ambitions were mixed up with the feeling of being isolated and undervalued," and, later, "I wanted to write enormous naturalistic novels with unhappy endings, full of detailed descriptions and arresting similes, and also full of purple passages in which words were used partly for the sake of their sound." Writing at this stage was for Orwell a kind of compensation, the creation of a private inner world. It also expressed his delusions of upward mobility, as his poetry reveals. At this early stage he wanted nothing more than to join the serene middle class of patriotic song and picturesque prose, a life which represented itself to him later as that of "a happy vicar . . . two hundred years ago."

His rude awakening from this dream occurred during his years as a lower-level colonial administrator in Burma, which position he describes with uncharacteristic euphemism as an "unsuitable profession." In fact, it was rather a job than a profession and unsuitable only in that very probably it did not match the professional fortunes of his classmates. In any case, and for some commendable reasons, it did not suit Orwell, and it probably also taught him that extreme contempt for bureaucratic language and empty formulae that marks his writing from then on.

There followed a period of poverty, half voluntary, half enforced, which brought a sense of failure as well as the tremendous political conscience that was to inform the rest of his writing life. At this point in his description of his development, Orwell begins to speak firmly of the primacy of content over form, of "truth" over "art." This is all very well, but at times it seems that he is here really rejecting not only his dreams of literary participation in a middle-class world, but the rich impulses behind them as well. There is a certain asceticism at work, a desire to reduce the motive of "sheer egoism" that he specifies as a part of all writers' make up. His work becomes at this time prompted more by external events than by his own direction: "When I sit down to write a book, I do not say to myself, 'I am going to produce a work of art.' I write because there is some lie that I want to expose, some fact to which I want to draw attention, and my initial concern is to get a hearing." Aesthetic considerations follow this motivation; they do not lead it, though Orwell of course would like to reconcile the two.

But if "no book is genuinely free of political bias," as Orwell rightly says, neither is any political bias entirely free from the demands of form. Too many protests about the primacy of "truth" over "art" may well mask an aesthetic and a politics of their own. In this context, the example Orwell cites from his own work is revealing. In *Homage to Catalonia*, he says, there is a long defense of Trotskyists accused of plotting with Franco. This digression breaks the flow of the narrative, but it is necessary because his outrage on their behalf gave Orwell the primary impulse to write. Actually, the digression does not break the form, but merely changes it—from poetic prose to journalism. It is that change of which Orwell speaks when he says he wants to write "less picturesquely and more exactly." Exactitude here means something very special, however. The fact is that Orwell's own particular biases (which have both political and aesthetic dimensions) lead him to defend the Trotskyists not for their political ideas or programs but for their innocence as particular persons accused of a particular crime. This reduction of a political group to a series of individuals necessitates a corresponding reduction in style, a reduction Orwell *chooses* to call "exactitude."

Each of these developments in Orwell's style represents, significantly, a step *down,* a "declassifying," in language, in content, and in social position as well. Through this descent Orwell becomes, as Terry Eagleton points out, the classic type of the lower-middle-class hero, forced to choose between inflated pretentions to bourgeois status and uneasy alliance with the working class. Orwell, to his credit, chooses the later course, but he never quite overcomes his social and linguistic unease with the result. He is very deeply tied to middle-class notions of style; "exactitude" in the case of *Homage to Catalonia* is not all that far from the detailed descriptive novels with unhappy endings he once wished to write. As a result, Orwell sees himself not only *moving* down but *writing* down, to an audience he only imperfectly understands. Given this position, history itself supplies the "unhappy ending."

Nowhere is this uneasy stance more evident than in "Marrakech," where problems of race, class, and language are involved in the content as well as the style of Orwell's work. Teaching this essay in a beginning composition course, especially one with a good number of minority students, is highly revealing both of Orwell and of the standard notions of what he is about. In one case, for example, I used this essay with a freshman class, introductory in level and just about equal in racial mix. (Often fifty-fifty is an ideal ratio in terms of race, as it seems to allow both black and white students a certain measure of security which leaves them free to participate.) The class had done very well with material as touchy as Baldwin's *The Fire Next Time* and as outrageously racist as Mailer's "The White Negro," both of which seemed to generate strong responses even in writing, which is rare. With Orwell, however, the reaction was silence, embarrassment, and a kind of deep confusion that seemed to produce nothing but apathy. Finally, when put to it, the class located its unease in two passages, both of which will bear analysis.

The first comes at the beginning of the piece where Orwell refers to the Jews in the ghetto in Marrakech:

> As a matter of fact, there are thirteen thousand of them, all living in the space of a few acres. A good job Hitler wasn't here. Perhaps he was on his way, however. You hear, the usual dark rumours about Jews, not only from the Arabs but from the poorer Europeans.
>
> "Yes, *mon vieux,* they took my job away from me and gave it to a Jew. The Jews! They're the real rulers of this country, you know. They've got all the money. They control the banks, finance, everything."

Here the embarrassment my students felt has, on one level, a perfectly simple explanation: their anti-Semitism (which is widely shared, as it seems more and more necessary lately to point out) coupled with their inability to "hear" irony, so that they found Orwell confirming their worst fears even when they knew this was unlikely to be the case. Such misreadings are important both for the real questions they raise and for the new readings skills they demand. In this case, however, an airing of these matters did not clear up the text, much less the minds of the class. Their confusion remained primary and carried over to the second passage, where misreading was unfortunately not the problem. Here Orwell is watching a regiment of black soldiers being marched off to fight in World War II. As the column goes by, Orwell catches the eye of a Senegalese private. The passage is narrated as follows:

> They were Senegalese, the blackest Negroes in Africa, so black that sometimes it is difficult to see whereabouts on their necks the hair begins. Their splendid bodies were hidden in reach-me-down khaki uniforms, their feet squashed into boots that looked like blocks of wood. . . . The curiously sensitive black faces were glistening with sweat.
>
> As they went past a tall, very young Negro turned and caught my eye. But the look he gave me was not in the least the kind of look you might expect. Not hostile, not contemptuous, not sullen, not even inquisitive. It was the shy, wide-eyed Negro look, which actually is a look of profound respect. I saw how it was. This wretched boy, who is a French citizen, and has therefore been dragged from the forest to scrub floors and catch syphilis in garrison towns, actually has feelings of reverence before a white skin. He has been taught that the white race are his masters, and he still believes it.

At many points in this little vignette the class positively writhed with embarrassment, and so, I confess, did I. This reaction was clearly deeper than a semantic mixup over the dated term "Negro" and came also from more than the usual racial tension that writing on this topic tends to produce. Nor does Orwell have the defense of the ironic style here. The tone is one of naïve wonder, and the irony is clearly placed in the situation, not in the narrative voice.

That situation is, however, partly of Orwell's own making. Here we have the spectacle of a white observer, in momentary contact with a black working-class soldier whose language he does not speak and whose coun-

try he does not know. Orwell so overreacts to this contact that he plunges
into the wildest speculations. Seconds after the soldier looks at him, Orwell
has provided him with a life history, a vocational and medical record, and
a psychological condition any part of which may or may not be true. Having invented these for the poor young man—who no doubt has troubles of
his own—Orwell proceeds to find himself depressed with the result and
forced to hypothesize a slur on the black man's intelligence as well. The
conclusion of the essay is quite extraordinary:

> But there is one thought which every white man (and in this
> connection it doesn't matter twopence if he calls himself a so-
> cialist) thinks when he sees a black army marching past. "How
> much longer can we go on kidding these people? How long be-
> fore they turn their guns in the other direction?"
>
> It was curious, really. Every white man there had this thought
> stowed away somewhere or other in his mind. I had it, so had
> the other onlookers, so had the officers on their sweating
> chargers and the white N.C.O.'s marching in the ranks. It was
> a kind of secret which we all knew and were too clever to tell;
> only the Negroes didn't know it. And really it was like watch-
> ing a flock of cattle to see the long column, a mile or two miles
> of armed men, flowing peacefully up the road, while the great
> white birds drifted over them in the opposite direction, glitter-
> ing like scraps of paper.

What is shocking here is not Orwell's fantasy, which indeed is a common one among whites, nor his commendable honesty in writing it down.
It is rather the extreme naïveté of his analysis. For a writer with some
claims to political consciousness, it is insupportable that he should assume
that "the shy, wide-eyed, Negro look" (as he so offensively calls it) con-
ceals nothing but respect, or indeed to think, given his distance from the
man's language and codes of behavior, that he can interpret that look at
all. Nor does he consider that the column of soldiers, moving like "a flock
of cattle" toward the north, may have made a rational estimate of their
own situation and quite correctly decided that this was no time for revolt.
(A South African friend recalls the mixture of anger and hilarity with
which Winston Churchill's speeches were heard by black people during
World War II. The political ironies of the "fight for democracy" were not
lost on that audience, and it is unlikely that they were any more beyond
the scope of the Senegalese.)

More difficult to get at here is the particular mixture of attraction and disgust toward black people that operates in this passage. The narrator shows a fascination with the physical details of their bodies—the hair, the skin—along with a sense of them as objects—"feet squashed into boots"—that is embarrassing in the extreme. Coupled with this curious, almost sexual objectification is a deep seated fear that informs almost all racist ideology, a fear of simple *numbers* of people. This fear is present even in the ironic defense of the Jews in the first passage, "thirteen thousand of them, all living in the space of a few acres." It is the particular combination of race *and* numbers, apparently, that makes human beings seem animal to Orwell and gives him that sense of "undifferentiated brown stuff, about as individual as bees or coral" that prepares for the "flock of cattle" image at the end.

Of course this sensibility is half-mocked by the narrator; it *is* ironic, as I kept trying to explain to the class. But there is a profound ambivalence as well, and a sense of psychic threat that is far more operative here than the rather unlikely possibility—in this context at least—of the guns being turned around. Freedom, for Orwell, lies finally with the brilliant image of the stark, white birds flying in the opposite direction from the masses, as disembodied and as few in number as the scraps of paper on which Hitler's treaties were made.

All of these points can be made, and made effectively, with students in a literature class. Models for writers, however, demand at minimum an ability on the part of the student to identify with the narrator and to pick up on his writing strategies and techniques. With Orwell such identification means not only a "privileging of the 'I' over the 'we' " but means it in a way that is threatening indeed. It is one thing, even for a white student, to identify with Baldwin's passionate, sexual, and emotional narrator in *The Fire Next Time*, with his remarkable ability to move back and forth between a personal and a public, even biblical style; and quite another for him to ally himself with Orwell's uneasy, isolated, and ambivalent "I," caught in conflicts he seems only barely to understand. To be "like Orwell" even for purposes of a composition, is for most students to objectify, reify, and speak "down" to the very class from which they come. The middle-class code, though by no means neutral, is surely more versatile than this.

Is there then a place for Orwell in the curriculum at all? The question is a real one, especially given his ubiquitous presence in composition texts and his relative absence from the literary scene. It is as if, now that the furor over his use as a stick to beat the communists has died down, Orwell has already been relegated to the dustbin of history. Now he lives only as a symbolic figure of the kind hypostatized by Lionel Trilling's student, who says with apparently artless simplicity, " 'he was a virtuous man.' " According to Trilling, the two of them then sit in the conference room "agreeing at length about this statement and finding pleasure in talking about it." Epitaphs like these are the ultimate exclusion, in that they relegate a writer to the status of those "silent and terroristic objects in the museum of modern culture" of which Fredric Jameson so eloquently warns.

The trouble is that, like any repressed content, Orwell haunts us still. If his work is biased in terms of class and race—and it is—then it also *intends not to be,* and, as Edward Said has shown, this intention is operative when we read. In his willingness to name class and race problems in his work and his conscious situation of writing in the context of a life of struggle, Orwell is valuable precisely for the debates he forces us to raise.

What we need is to apply to Orwell the kind of criticism Jameson calls *"working through."* We need to give his prose a reading that will "dissolve the reification of the great monumental works" and "return these artistic and academic 'monuments' to their original reality as the private languages of isolated individuals." Certainly an Orwell read in these terms, an Orwell presented critically in the context of students from a variety of class and race backgrounds, would be very different from the fifties relic we have before us now. Of course, the ultimate result of such a process might well be a certain diminishment of his work. Following Jameson's dream analogy, it may turn out that our interest in Orwell dissolves with analysis, just as our obsession with certain fantasies disappears once their roots become clear. For this to happen as a result of "just and fraternal evaluation," however, is one thing; for it to happen by a kind of benign neglect, even while we continue to administer doses of "Politics and the English Language" to our students, is quite another. Orwell deserves better than this kind of offhand patronage. If nothing else, his work must be taken seriously as a real praxis in the world, without shirking the judgments such consideration must entail.

ROY HARRIS

The Misunderstanding of Newspeak

Orwell and Ruskin did not, on the face of it, have much in common. But Ruskin once said something that Orwell might well have used as his motto for an Orwellian linguistics: "the greatest thing a human soul ever does in this world is to see something and tell what it saw in a plain way." That summarizes Orwell's theorizing about language, just as it summarizes Ruskin's theorizing about art. Let us call it the *doctrine of plain representation*. It has a simple, noble, fundamentalist ring to it.

The significance of "Newspeak," the most famous figment of Orwellian linguistics, cannot be understood without reference to the doctrine of plain representation. Ruskin was doubtless thinking primarily of pictorial representation, whereas Orwell was thinking of linguistic representation. They share, however, an important set of assumptions about the concept of representation itself. The Newspeak of Orwell's novel *1984* is a language which, for certain topics, makes plain representation in the verbal mode impossible. Newspeak, in short, stands the doctrine of plain representation on its head. The pictorial equivalent for Ruskin would have been a perverse mode of drawing ("Newdraw") in which, for example, all straight lines were automatically represented as curves or wiggles—anything, in fact, *other than* straight lines. Why any artistic Establishment should bother to devise such a distorted system of pictorial representation as Newdraw is, of course, puzzling. On the other hand, where language is concerned the motivation is allegedly less obscure: it is, quite bluntly, a

From *Times Literary Supplement* (January 6, 1984). © 1984 by *TLS,* London.

social and political motivation—a way of fooling most of the people most of the time.

It seems somehow significant that the term *Newspeak* itself, which Orwell introduced to the English-speaking world only thirty-five years ago, should in that relatively short time have undergone all or most of the socio-linguistic processes which validate it as part of the vocabulary of Old-speak. What does that show? Different things, according to taste. Some will argue that it shows Orwell's linguistic worries were basically ground-less, and that language obeys laws which scheming politicians and propa-gandists are powerless to interfere with. Others will argue, to the contrary, that it shows Orwell's linguistic instincts were basically sound, and that the subtle forms of ideological control to which the vocabulary of our public discourse is subject are powerful enough to neutralize the explosive poten-tial of new terms which directly challenge them.

What is less controversial is that in the process of assimilation into the vocabulary of Oldspeak the word *Newspeak* has undergone emasculation. A recently published dictionary of what purports to be Newspeak includes new-fangled professional jargon of any and every kind. That is not what Orwell meant. Newspeak is not Newspeak in virtue of being just new speak. Orwell was not so stupid as to think that Shakespeare had already anticipated every lexical requirement of computer-age English.

The Newspeak of *1984* is a deliberately distorted language, designed to ensure the political enslavement of its speakers. Its aim, as Orwell de-scribes it, is that thoughts not approved by the Party "should be literally unthinkable." That final horrendous vision at the end of the novel, where we are told the details of the programme by which Newspeak will eventu-ally replace Oldspeak entirely—that vision of how the deliberate manipula-tion of language could make freedom of thought impossible—remains one of the most chillingly powerful in the whole of English literature.

The Newspeak parable is a parable which strikes home to any audi-ence whose native language is English. For there is a sense in which the very variety and flexibility of English as a language seems to guarantee to its users their individual right to think and speak as they please. It is no accident of history that England has never had a body equivalent to the Académie Française. The notion of a language subject to the dictatorial control of experts is as repugnant to most English people as the idea of censorship. As people who can draw upon the resources of one of the rich-est vocabularies in the world, we can feel nothing but repulsion for the loathsome philologist from the Ministry of Truth in *1984* who says gloat-ingly: "It's a beautiful thing, the destruction of words."

Orwell's parable raises in a dramatic form what is a much wider issue for any community which takes this English view of linguistic freedom: the question of our social responsibilities as language-users. It is to Orwell's credit that he brought this question to the attention of a whole generation who might otherwise have overlooked it, or not been able to focus it clearly for themselves. It is all the more regrettable that his parable took the particular form it did. For Newspeak is, and is likely to remain, unsurpassed as a fictional portrayal of logophobia: and logophobia has become one of the most characteristic maladies of our times.

Certainly Orwell seems to have suffered from acute fits of it. He was not merely, as Anthony Burgess describes him, "a word-user who distrusted words" (so, to some extent, are we all) but one whose distrust of words at times bordered on the pathological. As a professional writer, he realized what he owed to his own skills of verbal manipulation. As a committed socialist, on the other hand, he instinctively disliked verbal skills as skills pre-eminently inculcated, valued and practised by a class-based educational system of which he disapproved (but of which he himself was a highly articulate product). Hence his unspoken fear that to practise verbal persuasion, to engage in verbal polemic even in the cause of socialism—or any "good" cause—might be to legitimize a trust in words which could ultimately be betrayed by words themselves. Newspeak was the public fantasy which gave fictional form to Orwell's private nightmare. But this fantasy has a psychological validity and cultural significance which go far beyond the particular circumstances of Orwell's dilemma.

Logophobia is not an exclusively twentieth-century phenomenon. It goes back at least as far as the Greek philosopher Cratylus, whose logophobia was so acute that eventually, we are told, he renounced the use of words as a mode of expression altogether. Orwell was by no means so desperate a case: he could not afford to be. What makes him such a typical representative of twentieth-century logophobia (as distinct from, say, the more esoteric logophobia of the early Wittgenstein or the more hindsighted variety of Marshall McLuhan) is his ultimate faith in the aforementioned doctrine of plain representation.

Orwellian logophobia is based on two interconnected doubts about the trustworthiness of the connection between words and meaning. One is that instead of revealing what is meant, words may be used to obscure or conceal it. The other is that instead of revealing what is meant, words may be used to misrepresent it. Hence the generalized form which Orwell's nightmare takes—the postulation of a language which has been "doctored" in such a way as to deceive its users systematically about certain social and political aspects of the world in which they live, and further-more, "doctored" in such a way as to make it impossible for the language-users themselves to detect the deception.

The fears underlying this logophobic extrapolation are based on Or-well's disgust at instances of what he saw as linguistic dishonesty and de-ception. This revulsion comes out strongly in some of his most vigorous writing. "Defenceless villages are bombarded from the air, the inhabitants driven out into the countryside, the cattle machine-gunned, the huts set on fire with incendiary bullets; this is called *pacification*." The Vietnam gener-ation did not need to find the words: Orwell had already said it for them.

Unfortunately, Orwell's abhorrence of the way man's inhumanity to man can be concealed behind all kinds of verbal façades led him to make an erroneous diagnosis. He thought that there was something going wrong with the English language of his day. His essay on "Politics and the English Language" makes this perfectly clear. "Most people who bother with the matter at all," he wrote, "would admit that the English language is in a bad way, but it is generally assumed that we cannot by conscious action do anything about it." Orwell believed that something could and should be done about it; but what he proposed to do simply showed how shallow his thinking about language was, and how uncritically he swallowed the doctrine of plain representation. He inveighed against the "bad influence" of American usage and its "debasing effect." He condemned expressions which he considered to betray "slovenliness," "ugliness," "lack of preci-sion," "meaninglessness," and "pretentious diction." One of his recom-mendations was to memorize the sentence "A not unblack dog was chasing a not unsmall rabbit across a not ungreen field." In short, he showed ex-actly the same prescriptivist attitudes towards language as can be found in most published guides to "correct" usage, or any representative selection of complaints to the BBC about the decline of contemporary "standards" of English. Orwell attacks, as one essay on him puts it, "most of the mis-uses of language that have become the favourites of indignant letter-writers of any persuasion."

It would be misguided to defend Orwell by trying to distinguish his progressive and radical approach to questions of usage from the conserva-tive, reactionary inspiration of the majority of "indignant letter-writers." The plain fact is that Orwell's attitude was no more enlightened than theirs. Accusing one's political opponents of "perverting the English lan-guage" is a game that both right and left can play, as recent arguments about nuclear weapons and unilateral disarmament have all too clearly shown. The fact that in the view of many observers the left emerged victorious from that particular fracas should not be misinterpreted. Appeal to the doctrine of plain representation is a double-edged weapon. To those inclined to think otherwise I would recommend consideration of two 1983 examples where the concept of Newspeak is invoked under the banner of writers not notorious (*pace* Orwell) for their left-wing sympathies.

The first is provided by an article in the *Times* entitled "How Newspeak Leaves Us Naked" (February 1, 1983), in which Roger Scruton uses a criticism of the definitions provided by the Moscow Novosti Press Agency's *Short Guide to Political Terms* (which countenances "democracy" as genuine only when understood as preceded by the adjective "socialist" and definitionally underwritten by the "dictatorship of the proletariat") as a springboard for an attack upon feminism. Feminism is described as "an ideology which, like communism, seeks to abolish history, to abolish human nature, and to abolish every thought which conflicts with its dominant and erroneous idea—the idea of the moral indistinguishability of men and women." Feminism, the article continues, "seeks to appropriate not only vocabulary, but also grammar, and to eliminate gender from a language structured by gender distinctions." (This is presumably a reference to controversies about using the masculine pronoun as the unmarked anaphoric form in sentences like *No one ought to forget his linguistic obligations to the community.*)

My second example is Friedrich von Hayek's onslaught on the phrase *social justice* (the *Times*, November 11, 1983). Hayek endorses Charles Curran's condemnation of this expression as "a semantic fraud from the same stable as People's Democracy," and describes the adjective *social* as "probably the most confusing and misleading term of our whole political vocabulary." The villain of the piece is Rousseau, apparently, in whose *Contrat Social* the wretched term "appears as an essential part of the rhetorical substitute for conventional morals." *Social*, in short, is castigated by Hayek as a "weasel word"; and a weasel word is described as a word "used to draw the teeth from a concept which one is obliged to employ, but from which one wishes to eliminate all implications that challenge one's ideological premises." The reader might perhaps have more confidence in this description were it not that this condemnation appears under a caption which advertises "F. A. Hayek on Newspeak exemplified". Does that make *Newspeak* itself a weasel word? And if so, which word shall escape whipping? Logophobia is evidently not a disease confined to any particular segment of the political spectrum.

In case the juxtaposition of these two examples might tend to cause apoplexy in some readers, perhaps it is worth interjecting a disclaimer. There is, indeed, a distinction to be drawn between the political ranting of a Scruton and the political rationale of a Hayek. The point, however, is that both can use the doctrine of plain representation for their own purposes: and for every Scruton or Hayek there will be an Orwell or an Orwellian to complain about the other side's use of expressions like *pacification, nuclear deterrent,* and *acceptable casualties.* Propaganda always lays claim to a linguistic monopoly of truth.

The real misrepresentations which are central to these arguments and counter-arguments are not abuses of the English language at all. They are much more fundamental. They are abuses of our concept of a language itself. The reason why there could be no such language as Orwell's Newspeak is identical with the reason why there could be no such language as the idealized Oldspeak to which it stands opposed. No language can ever give us "plain representation," and it is an intellectual deception to imply that we should expect it to. The doctrine of plain representation is simply linguistic utopianism. Like all forms of utopianism, it provides countless traps for the simple-minded and endless claptrap for charlatans to exploit.

As the real—rather than the fictional—1984 arrives, we find the English-speaking community in a comical-tragical state of legislative turmoil over questions of "plain language." On one side of the Atlantic, British farmers are not allowed to call fresh milk "fresh" when it has come straight from the cow. Why not? Paradoxically, *because* it has come straight from the cow. (It may, of course, become "fresh" two days later, having been pasteurized in the interim.) Meanwhile on the other side of the Atlantic, we find states all over America rushing in legislation to protect the common man against the complexities of Oldspeak. Such enactments require, for example, that "every consumer contract shall be written in a clear and coherent manner using words with common and everyday meanings." But over the rather crucial questions of which words actually have "common and everyday meanings" and how we are supposed to know exactly what these "common and everyday meanings" are, the plain-language legislators wisely draw the discreet semantic veil of silence.

For Orwell, it would doubtless be one of the ironies of history that the country which took the lead in "defending" its Vietnam policy externally by means of Newspeak should now take the lead in defending the rights of its own proletariat to use Oldspeak for internal domestic purposes. But the irony is not to be laid at history's door: it is a projection from Orwell's own misconceptions about the way linguistic communication works.

Calling a spade a spade is not something languages can do: only language-users. And if language-users do not like the word *spade*, or cannot make it mean what they want to, then they will make another, with or without government intervention. Orwell's classic series of mistakes was to suppose (1) that something called "the English language" lays down the true meaning of a word like *spade*; (2) that words like *spade* mean what they say; and (3) that anything which needs to be said can be said using words like *spade*—in short, by using words any ordinary man can understand because the words in question directly reflect a recognizable reality. This muddled complex of beliefs has become one of the most popular pieces of linguistic folklore of modern times. It was Orwell's naïve commitment to that folklore which led to his creation of the fictional antilanguage of Newspeak, and hence to his (deserved) canonization as a prophet of twentieth-century culture.

GEORGE WOODCOCK

George Orwell and the Living Word

Like every good writer, George Orwell was concerned from the beginning, in a rather general way, with the problem of language, of how to express an idea or recreate a scene in felicitous and true words. But what distinguished him from many other writers was his early concern with the public use of language—language as an instrument of persuasion—into which he was led by the political and polemical interests that made him what he described as "a sort of pamphleteer." In the early days there was indeed another Orwell—the writer of novels like *Burmese Days* and *Keep the Aspidistra Flying*—who was tempted towards writing what he called "enormous naturalistic novels with unhappy endings, full of detailed descriptions and arresting similes, and also full of purple passages in which words were used partly for the sake of their sounds." But very early in his career Orwell approached the ideal he tried to fulfill in his later years when he said (in "Why I Write," 1946): "I write because there is some lie that I want to expose, some fact to which I want to draw attention, and my initial concern is to get a hearing."

This inclination emerged already in his early essay "A Hanging" (1931), in which he described in clear and simple terms an incident whose wider implications—the immorality of the death penalty—he wished to draw to the attention of his readers. There is none of his books written after his period of fighting in Spain (1936–37) in which one is not aware that the inventive faculty is very much controlled by the polemical urge. Indeed, the best of Orwell's prose, given his special polemical talent, was

From *Queen's Quarterly* 91, no. 3 (Autumn 1984). © 1984 by George Woodcock.

that which he wrote with a didactic intent. He himself said in "Why I Write" that "where I lacked a *political* purpose . . . I wrote lifeless books, and was betrayed into purple passages, sentences without meaning, decorative adjectives and humbug generally."

At the same time, Orwell drew very sharply the distinction between the kind of political writing he saw himself producing and propaganda written in the cause of a party. As he remarked in many of his great essays—notably "The Prevention of Literature"—no writing can be good when the writer does not produce it in an atmosphere of intellectual and moral freedom, which does not exist if one writes in response to the dictates of a party, no matter how congenial one may find its general attitude. The writer should say what he feels he must "as an individual, an outsider, at the most an unwelcome guerrilla on the flank of a regular army."

The question of the independence of the writer from political connections as distinct from political inclinations was itself connected with language. For, as Orwell pointed out, there are many occasions when logic or experience drive a writer to "a conclusion which is perfectly plain but which can only be drawn if one is privately disloyal to the official ideology." In such a case, "the normal response is to push the question, unanswered, into a corner of one's mind, and then continue repeating contradictory catchwords." And catchwords—as we shall later see Orwell repeatedly declaring—clog the language by defeating the aim of clarity. For Orwell the search for political honesty and for clarity of expression went hand-in-hand. He remarked in 1946 that "of late years I have tried to write less picturesquely and more exactly," and he added his famous maxim: "Good prose is like a window pane."

If Orwell thought that political honesty and clear thinking went with a prose based on an exact and supple use of the language, he also believed that the corruption of the language went with the corruption of political manners, and that manipulation of the language was one of the most effective instruments in the hands of a tyranny seeking to abolish freedom. This view of course reached its peak with the part played by the invention of "Newspeak" in *1984* and its use to banish from the minds of the people any thoughts other than those approved by the ruling party of Oceania.

The interest in language was present throughout Orwell's literary career, though it was not until the 1940s, the last decade of his life, that it assumed a special importance in his criticism and in his political thinking. From his early days as a writer he was interested in special forms of language, perhaps not in dialects, but certainly in subdialects. There are glossaries of tramps' slang in his first book *Down and Out in Paris and Lon-*

don and of cockney slang in "Hop-Picking," the diary of his experiences in the Kentish hopfields that was written in 1931 but first published in 1968 in the *Collected Essays, Journalism and Letters of George Orwell.*

In the novels that followed *Burmese Days* during the 1930s Orwell was exploring the social falsities of British society, particularly in *A Clergyman's Daughter* and *Keep the Aspidistra Flying,* with political criticism making its appearance in *Coming Up for Air.* In the last two novels the corrupting of the language with the aim of deceiving readers or listeners plays a notable part.

In *Keep the Aspidistra Flying,* Gordon Comstock is a bookshop assistant who formerly worked for the New Albion advertising agency.

> At that time they were working on a line of magazine ads for April Dew, the great new deodorant which the Queen of Sheba Toilet Requisites Co. . . . were putting on the market. Gordon started on the job with secret loathing. But now there was a quite unexpected development. It was that Gordon showed, almost from the start, a remarkable talent for copywriting. He could compose an ad as though he had been born to it. The vivid phrase that sticks and rankles, the neat little para. that packs a world of lies into a hundred words—they came to him almost unsought. He had always had a gift for words, but this was the first time he had used it successfully. . . . Gordon watched his own development, first with surprise, then with amusement, and finally with a kind of horror. *This,* then, was what he was coming to! Writing lies to tickle the money out of fools' pockets! There was a beastly irony, too, in the fact that he, who wanted to be a "writer," should score his sole success in writing ads for deodorants. However, that was less unusual than he imagined. Most copywriters, they say, are novelists *manqués;* or is it the other way about?

In such passages one sees Orwell's realization of the double aspects of the gift of words. It can be used to create words of art and enlightenment; it can also be used to deceive and defraud. Sometimes the borderline between the good and the bad use of words can be a very slender one.

Gordon rebels not only against his occupation of manipulating words, but also against the whole philosophy of Making Good at the expense of others and against the world which the advertisement business represents at its worst. He tries to lose himself in the underworld of anonymous poverty, but he does not succeed. For *Keep the Aspidistra Flying,* like all of

Orwell's works of fiction, is ultimately a book about failure and survival, and Gordon is dragged back by his love of Rosemary into a limbo of domesticity whose maintenance required that he surrender and return to the New Albion.

Back there he works once again on the Queen of Sheba advertisements, giving a fresh slant to the April Dew campaign. His new superior, fresh from Madison Avenue, invents P.P. or "pedic perspiration" as a bogey to frighten readers into buying the deodorant; the word "pedic" is in no dictionary, but that does not matter to the advertisers so long as the readers feel "a guilty terror."

> It was Mr Warner who supplied the bold sweeping ideas, sketched the general layout of the ads, and decided what pictures would be needed; but it was Gordon who wrote most of the letterpress—wrote the harrowing little stories, each a realistic novel in a hundred words, about despairing virgins of thirty, and lonely bachelors and overworked wives who could not afford to change their stockings once a week and who saw their husbands subsiding into the clutches of "the other women." He did it very well; he did it far better than he had ever done anything else in his life. Mr Warner gave golden reports of him. There was no doubt about Gordon's literary ability. He could use words with the economy that is only learned by years of effort. So perhaps his long agonizing struggles to be a "writer" had not been wasted after all.

Orwell's writing was full of anticipations, and in Gordon Comstock sitting in the offices of New Albion and manipulating words as part of a business devoted entirely to fooling the public, we get an anticipatory glimpse of the Ministry of Truth in *1984,* which is devoted entirely to the manufacture and spreading of lies, and in which Winston Smith, working in one of the many departments, uses his gift for words to rewrite history according to the constant changes in the party line.

In *Keep the Aspidistra Flying* Orwell is attacking the general practice of misusing words for commercial purposes so that they deceive instead of enlightening; he does not attempt a close examination of specific instances, and we are given only some very brief examples of the kind of pernicious nonsense Gordon actually writes. In *Coming Up for Air* the concern over the manipulation of words, both commercial and political, is there as strongly as before—perhaps even more strongly because of Orwell's experience in Spain—but since the leading character George Bowling, unlike Gordon Comstock, is not a professional user of words, his statements are less explicit, though there is one passage, when Bowling attends a Left Book Club lecture in his jerry-built suburb, that clearly anticipates the later essays which discuss how political ways of thinking turn language into lifeless slogans whose deadness in turn infects the very process of thinking and inhibits the emergence of independent ideas.

> At the beginning I wasn't exactly listening. The lecturer was rather a mean looking little chap, but a good speaker. White face, very mobile mouth and the rather grating voice that they get from constant speaking. Of course he was pitching into Hitler and the Nazis. I wasn't particularly keen to hear what he was saying—get the same stuff in the *News Chronicle* every morning—but his voice came across to me as a kind of burr-burr-burr, with now and again a phrase that struck out and caught my attention.
>
> "Bestial atrocities . . . Hideous outbursts of sadism . . . Rubber truncheons . . . Concentration camps . . . Iniquitous persecution of the Jews . . . Back to the Dark Ages . . . European civilization. . . . Act before it is too late . . . Indignation of all decent peoples . . . Alliance of the democratic nations . . . Firm stand . . . Defence of democracy . . . Democracy . . . Fascism . . . Democracy . . . Fascism . . . Democracy . . . "
>
> You know the line of talk. These chaps can churn it out by the hour. Just like a gramophone. Turn the handle, press the button, and it starts. Democracy, Fascism, Democracy. But somehow it interested me to watch him. A rather mean little man, with a white face and a bald head, standing on a platform, shooting out slogans. What's he doing? Quite deliberately, and quite openly, he's stirring up hatred. Doing his damnedest to make you hate certain foreigners called Fascists. It's a queer thing, I thought, to be known as "Mr So-and-so, the well-known anti-Fascist." A queer trade, anti-Fascism. This fellow, I suppose, makes his living by writing books against Hitler. But what did he do before Hitler came along? And what'll he do if Hitler ever disappears? Same question applies to doctors, detectives, rat-catchers, and so forth, of course. But the grating voice went on and on, and another thought struck me. He *means* it. Not faking at all—feels every word he's saying. He's trying to work up hatred in the audience, but that's

nothing to the hatred he feels himself. Every slogan's gospel truth to him. If you cut him open all you'd find inside would be Democracy-Fascism-Democracy. Interesting to know a chap like that in private life. But does he have a private life? Or does he only go round from platform to platform, working up hatred? Perhaps even his dreams are slogans.

Of course, Orwell is speaking here through an idiosyncratic character, a kind of ideal plain man, but the point to be made is that he is not excusing fascism or abandoning democracy; he is pointing out that if we allow our thoughts on this or any other political question to settle into the linguistic groove of sloganizing, we are abandoning the independence of mind that we need to combat social evils.

Ironically, during World War II, when Orwell's awakened patriotism made him want to fight for his country, his poor health, following on a bout of tuberculosis in 1938, meant that the only war work he could find was in the British Broadcasting Corporation, where he arranged radio programs that disseminated British propaganda to India. I knew him then, and how quickly he became disillusioned. "You don't realize what muck and filth is flowing through the air," he wrote to me. He finally left the BBC late in 1943, and it is significant that almost immediately afterwards he showed a great concern for language and its misuse, especially in political writing, and an equal desire to refine his own use of language so that it became accessible as possible, which meant making it more colloquial than is usual in literary writing, and as exact as possible, which meant a constant struggle against writing for effect and against unnecessary complexity.

It is true that here and there in the early 1940s Orwell was exposing instances of the slovenly use of language—sometimes a deliberately slovenly use as in the Communists' habit of using the word "Trotskyist" (or alternatively "Fascist") to define almost anyone who did not share their beliefs, without regard for the particular appropriateness of the epithet. There is also a curious essay, entitled "New Words," unpublished until it was included in the *Collected Essays, Journalism and Letters* (1968) but conjecturally dated 1940, in which he talked of "reforming language," of finding ways of extending its range so as to express the widening range of emotions stirred up by modern living.

> At present, as Samuel Butler said, the best art (i.e. the most perfect thought-transference) must be "lived" from one person to another. It need not be so if our language were more adequate.

> It is curious that when our knowledge, the complication of our lives and therefore (I think it must follow) our minds, develop so fast, language, the chief means of communication, should scarcely stir.

The idea of reforming the language remained lodged in Orwell's mind, though when he made fictional use of it at the end of the 1940s, it would be in a negative way, since the Party in *1984* reforms the language so that its range of expression is not extended but minimized.

In 1944, the year after Orwell left the BBC, his broadened interest in language emerged in a number of texts. Perhaps the most important was *The English People,* a small book published in 1944 that contains a chapter devoted to "The English Language." Here Orwell notes the "outstanding characteristics" of the English language as "a very large vocabulary and simplicity of grammar." From this combination came its great virtues and its great faults.

> The greatest quality of English is its enormous range not only of meaning but of *tone.* It is capable of endless subtleties, and of everything from the most high-flown rhetoric to the most brutal coarseness. On the other hand, its lack of grammar makes it easily compressible. It is the language of lyric poetry, and also of headlines. On its lower levels it is very easy to learn, in spite of its irrational spelling. It can also for international purposes be reduced to very simple pidgin dialects, ranging from Basic to the "Bêche-de-mer" English used in the South Pacific. It is therefore well suited to be a world lingua franca, and it has in fact spread more widely than any other language.

At the same time, English has a great capacity for debasement: "Just because it is so easy to use, it is easy to use *badly.*" Because it is a language without reliable rules, writing, or even speaking it "is not a science but an art," and whoever writes it is in danger of endless pitfalls: "He is struggling against vagueness, against obscurity, against the lure of the decorative adjective, against the encroachment of Latin and Greek, and, above all, against the worn-out phrases and dead metaphors with which the language is cluttered up."

English, moreover, is "peculiarly subject to jargons"—the ways of speech and writing of special groups, notably officials, scientists and political theorists. But worst of all, in Orwell's view, is the "dreary dialect" called "standard English," which is utilized by newspaper editors, bureaucrats, radio announcers, and parliamentary speakers. It is characterized by its "reliance on ready-made phrases," and here Orwell gives one of those lists he began to enjoy making, lists of locutions that "may once have been fresh and vivid, but have now become mere thought-saving devices, having the same relation to living English as a crutch has to a leg": "*in due course, take the earliest opportunity, warm appreciation, deepest regret, explore every avenue, ring the changes, take up the cudgels, legitimate assumption, the answer is in the affirmative, etc. etc. . . . "*

Orwell balances the dangers of Latinization, which tends to ossify a mobile and wide-ranging language like English, with the perils of Americanization, which tends to reduce it. He argues that "to adopt the American language whole-heartedly would probably mean a huge loss of vocabulary. For though American produces vivid and witty turns of speech, it is terribly poor in names for natural objects and localities."

Orwell ends this chapter on the English language by reflecting his own efforts to create a colloquial writing language through drawing largely on everyday demotic English when he declares that "Language ought to be the joint creation of poets and manual workers, and in modern England it is difficult for these two classes to meet. When they can do so again—as, in a different way, they could in the feudal past—English may show more clearly than at present its kinship with the language of Shakespeare and Defoe."

I have devoted a good deal of attention to this rather short chapter of *The English People,* one of Orwell's least remembered books, because in one way or another it sketches out all the linguistic themes he was to develop in the brief but brilliant remainder of his life—the five years from 1944 to 1949, when he became too sick to continue writing.

Shortly before *The English People* was published, Orwell had left the British Broadcasting Corporation to become the literary editor of a left socialist paper, *Tribune.* Apart from his editing, Orwell for several years wrote in *Tribune* a series of brief articles under the general title of "As I Please," musing on incidents that had attracted his attention or thoughts that had passed through his mind. It was occasional essay-writing in the tradition that goes back through English literature via Hazlitt and Lamb to Addison and Steele in the early seventeenth century. Orwell wrote these little pieces quickly, on impulse, and often included the substance of conversations he had just had with his friends. Thus they were fresh in flavor and informal in approach, yet they were almost always didactic, trying to lodge some thought about life or the world in the minds of his socialist readers.

It was natural that his current preoccupations with language should find their way into the various items of "As I Please," and in the spring of 1944 there are many references that develop ideas already presented in *The English People*. On March 10, for example, he puts his assiduous reading of Communist pamphlets to use when he denounces "the dead metaphors and ill-translated foreign phrases that have been current in Marxist literature for years past," and adds yet another list of linguistic horrors going all the way from "Achilles' heel" and "jackboot" to "hyena" and "blood-bath." For the moment he does not develop the idea beyond remarking that "Marxist English, or Pamphletese," as he calls it, "is a style of writing that bears the same relation to writing real English as doing a jigsaw puzzle bears to painting a picture. It is just a question of fitting together a number of ready-made phrases. Just talk about hydra-headed jackboots riding roughshod over blood-stained hyenas, and you are all right."

A week later, Orwell was busy examining that excessively used term "Fascism" which, he remarked, on the one hand defined a specific "political and economic system," and on the other was pejoratively applied by their opponents to conservatives, socialists, Catholics, Trotskyists, and even to the Communists themselves, who used the word most freely in this way against their own opponents.

> It will be seen that, as used, the word "Fascism" is almost entirely meaningless. In conversation, of course, it is used even more wildly than in print. I have heard it applied to farmers, shopkeepers, Social Credit, corporal punishment, fox-hunting, bull-fighting, the 1922 Committee, the 1941 Committee, Kipling, Gandhi, Chiang Kai-shek, homosexuality, Priestley's broadcasts, Youth Hostels, astrology, women, dogs and I do not know what else.

Orwell seems to conclude that the issue is too befogged for a satisfactory definition of Fascism to be reached that all political factions will accept: "All one can do for the moment is to use the word with a certain amount of circumspection and not, as is usually done, degrade it to the level of a swearword." Orwell would have noted with sardonic amusement that even today, when the historic Fascist movement has long receded into the past, people of various political orientations are still happily using it to abuse each other, perhaps with greater satisfaction because of its complete irrelevancy in the late twentieth century.

In the following months Orwell wrote in his "As I Please" column on the excessive use of foreign phrases in English (why say *"cul-de-sac"* when "blind alley" already exists and is more expressive?); on "wornout and useless metaphors" (which he claims are favored by people who "evidently don't attach any definite meaning to the words they use"); and on Basic English, whose simplicity he then thought might be "a sort of corrective to the oratory of statesmen and publicists." (Later he was to shift his point of view and in *1984* to represent any simplification of the language as a dangerous weapon in the hands of totalitarian regimes.) He did not even spare himself from criticism. In "As I Please" on January 17, 1947 he wrote:

> Looking back through what I have written above, I notice that I have used the phrase "a totally different person." For the first time it occurs to me what a stupid expression this is. As though there could be such a thing as a partially different person! I shall try to cut this phrase (and also "a very different person" and "a different person altogether") out of my vocabulary from now onwards.

Such passages show how continuous was Orwell's search for exactitude in phrasing and argument. But the remarks he made on language and its misuse in these periodical columns can perhaps best be regarded as notes for the larger essays he wrote on the relationship between the abuse of language and the prevention of literature and thought, and eventually of course for *1984,* in which the relationship between the impoverishment of the language and the total destruction of freedom is most elaborately explored.

A curious intermediary piece between the "As I Please" comments and the longer essays is "Propaganda and Demotic Speech." This long article, published in a magazine called *Persuasion,* is obviously a by-product of Orwell's broadcasting years, and on the surface it reads as an examination of propaganda techniques whose author recommends how much more effectively the use of direct speech can transmit a political message than the kind of circumlocutory verbiage generally used by politicians, who seem set on avoiding the use of "clear, popular everyday language." In this essay Orwell seems to stand at a crucial point in his reasoning. He clearly has some lingering faith in the *intentions* of democratic politicians, and assumes that their remoteness from ordinary people is due to an ignorance of the techniques of communication. It was only later, and reluctantly, that he came to realize that the lack of clarity in political statement may be as deliberately used to obscure the truth among democrats as it is among totalitarians. "Propaganda and Demotic Speech" shows a still slightly be-

wildered plain man defining his political orientation in the mid-twentieth-
century world. Perhaps the most significant fact about the essay is that
here Orwell clearly conceives the possibility of a democratic socialism that
had nothing to hide from the people and is therefore free to use with impu-
nity the "clear, popular everyday language" from which politicians usually
shy away.

The three great essays Orwell wrote on the theme of the prevention
of literature and thought were "The Prevention of Literature" and "Politics and the English Language," both published in 1946, and "Writers and
Leviathan," which appeared in 1948 and—apart from "Reflections on
Gandhi"—was the last of Orwell's major polemical pieces.

Each of these essays has its own obliquity. "The Prevention of Literature," written in high disillusionment after a P.E.N. Club conference cele-
brating the tercentenary of Milton's *Areopagitica,* is concerned only indirectly with language, though the right of free speech which Orwell here
defends obviously embraces the right to use language imaginatively and
creatively. "The Prevention of Literature" is really an extension of the re-
proaches Orwell levelled at English left-leaning intellectuals, and especially
those in charge of the media, who deliberately distorted and suppressed
the truth in the interests of the Communist cause, at the time of the Spanish Civil War. He found a remnant of the same attitude nearly a decade
later, at the post-war P.E.N. conference, where many of the delegates
seemed to assume that, while the writer should be dutifully anti-Fascist, he
should be prevented as far as possible from being anti-Communist, or at
least from talking about his anti-Communism. European intellectuals continued to hold on to the Russian connection longer than their political
leaders, who in the 1940s were busily shedding the political friendships
convenient in the war years.

Orwell had believed ever since about 1938 that the intellectuals (from
whose ranks he tended always by some curious logic to except himself)
were especially attracted to totalitarian ways of thinking, and that this was
one of the reasons for the impoverishment of European literature in his
age.

> But the history of totalitarian societies, or of groups of people
> who have adopted the totalitarian outlook, suggests that loss of
> liberty is inimical to all forms of literature. German literature
> almost disappeared during the Hitler regime, and the case was
> not much better in Italy. Russian literature, so far as one can
> judge by translations, has deteriorated markedly since the early
> days of the Revolution, though some of the verse seems to be

better than the prose. Few if any Russian novels that it is possible to take seriously have been translated for about fifteen years. In western Europe and America large sections of the literary intelligentsia have either passed through the Communist Party or been warmly sympathetic to it, but this whole leftward movement has produced extraordinarily few books worth reading.

Making a glancing anticipation of Julia, the heroine of *1984*—"It would probably not be beyond human ingenuity to write books by machinery"—Orwell goes on to show the ways in which "a sort of mechanizing process" already enters into media like film and radio (the age of television had not yet begun), and ends with the conclusion that:

> literature is doomed if liberty of thought perishes. Not only is it doomed in any country which retains a totalitarian structure; but any writer who adopts the totalitarian outlook, who finds excuses for persecution and the falsification of reality, thereby destroys himself as a writer. There is no way out of this. No tirades against "individualism" and the "ivory tower," no pious platitudes to the effect that "true individuality is only attained through identification with the community," can get over the fact that a bought mind is a spoiled mind. Unless spontaneity enters at some point or another, literary creation is impossible, and language itself becomes ossified.

So, almost as an afterthought, language finally enters the picture, but the implications of its late appearance in the essay should not be ignored. Literature, it is obvious to everyone, is dependent on a living language; it is a less recognized but equal truth that language, to keep growing and alive, needs to be fed by a vital literature.

Having considered literature with only this final explicit reference to language, Orwell changes the pattern in "Politics and the English Language" by considering language without explicit reference to literature. At the end of the essay he remarks: "I have not here been considering the literary use of language, but merely language as an instrument for expressing and not for concealing or preventing thought." In fact, in this essay where Orwell considers the way politicians and publicists misuse the language, literature is as strongly present by implication as language was in "The Prevention of Literature." For, given that Orwell believed in the political content of all literature in our time, it is impossible for him to attack the obfuscatory language of politicians without indirectly attacking the unnecessarily obscure language of poets or novelists dominated by aestheticism or by plain affectation.

"Politics and the English Language," which has long been a standard text in university English courses and schools of journalism, gathers together and subjects to deeper analysis all the various crimes against the clarity of language which Orwell had attacked piecemeal in his "As I Please" columns, shows how the deliberately inexact or evasive ways of using language become means of avoiding and ultimately preventing thought, and ends up in a series of recommendations or rules for the writing of clear English that embodies the principles of good prose by which, certainly in the period from *Homage to Catalonia* onwards, he had operated.

   i Never use a metaphor, simile or other figure of speech which you are used to seeing in print.
  ii Never use a long word where a short one will do.
 iii If it is possible to cut a word out, always cut it out.
  iv Never use the passive where you can use the active.
   v Never use a foreign phrase, a scientific word or a jargon word if you can think of an everyday English equivalent.
  vi Break any of these rules sooner than say anything outright barbarous.

"Writers and Leviathan" again edges away from language as the central subject to consider the writer in his relation to politics. Working on the essay just after he had completed the first draft of *1984*, Orwell felt impelled to contemplate the inevitability of politics playing a greater part in literature than it had done in any past age.

> Of course, the invasion of literature by politics was bound to happen. It must have happened, even if the special problem of totalitarianism had never arisen, because we have developed a sort of compunction which our grandfathers did not have, an awareness of the enormous injustice and misery of the world, and a guilt-stricken feeling that one ought to be doing something about it, which makes a purely aesthetic attitude towards life impossible. No one, now, could devote himself to literature as single-mindedly as Joyce or Henry James.

How is the writer to extricate himself from this situation? Not, clearly, by withdrawing from politics, which, in any real way, has become impossible in the modern world, but by refusing to adhere to any orthodoxy, by refusing to allow the political bosses to dictate to him, which means, virtually, by refusing to become a loyal party member. But this does not mean that he need become politically inactive or neutral: "There is no reason why he should not write in the most crudely political way, if he wishes to. Only he should do so as an individual, an outsider, at the most an unwelcome guerrilla on the flank of a regular army." Orwell ends with a comparison between writers and other political activists, showing the special kind of corruption that awaits writers who accept the dictates of the party bosses.

> For most people, the problem does not arise in the same form, because their lives are split already. They are truly alive only in their leisure hours, and there is no emotional connection between their work and their political activities. Nor are they generally asked, in the name of political loyalty, to debase themselves as workers. The artist, and especially the writer, is asked just that—in fact, it is the only thing that politicians ever ask of him.

The general slant of "Writers and Leviathan" is clearly thematic, concerned with *what* the writer has to say rather than *how* he will say it, though if we read this essay in conjunction with Orwell's other writings of this period about the relationship between literature and politics, we realize that the question of language is again implicit, since accepting a political orthodoxy means accepting the ways of speaking and writing that go with it. One could not write for a Communist periodical of the 1930s or 1940s like *Inprecor* or *The Daily Worker* without accepting a debased language, designed to deceive and evade.

The ideas Orwell developed in the various "As I Please" items and in the larger essays I have discussed formed an important part of his thought and conversation from early 1944 to the end of his active writing life—i.e. the period from the completion of *Animal Farm* until the completion of *1984*. Orwell was secretive about his books until the day of publication, and I know of none of his friends who had any idea of the actual plot of *1984* until it finally appeared. But the themes of the book formed part of his customary conversation at this time, and they were, essentially, the threat of a permanent totalitarian order created by the division of the world into a number of permanent spheres of influence, and the threat to the imaginative and creative life, and to thought itself, posed by totalitarian politics, which by definition invades every corner of people's lives.

1984 is a strange mixture of plots and themes and literary approaches. It owes its power to the neo-Gothic terror of Winston's torture and mental destruction, and its pathos to the romance of the doomed love of Winston Smith and Julia. But it owes its originality less to its vision of the political structure of the world to come, which takes a great deal from the nonfictional writings of James Burnham, than to a recognition that the one way to make a tyranny complete and lasting would be—as the rulers did in Zamiatin's *We*—to destroy the imagination, and that the imagination might most effectively be destroyed, not by a brain operation—again as in *We*—but by two means: taking over the past, so that it is constantly being rewritten to suit the policies of the present, and reforming language to the extent that it will become too restricted to stimulate ideas or allow for their expression, at which point independent thought will virtually come to an end.

The centrality of this idea in the novel is shown by the fact that of the four ministries in the future state of Oceania (Love, Truth, Plenty, Peace), only two play any important role in the novel. The Ministry of Love is the headquarters of the dreaded Thought Police, who seek out "thoughtcrime," the harboring of heretical ideas in the recesses of the mind, which is basically the only crime in Oceania, from which all errors and misdemeanors stem. But preventing the crime of independent thinking is as important as eliminating it, and the Ministry of Truth is devoted to the production of propaganda of every conceivable kind, including the machinewriting of pulp novels in which Julia is employed and the falsification of history which is Winston Smith's occupation. Precisely because the comparison of fact and fiction cannot always be avoided in its work, the Ministry of Truth is a perilous place to work, since doubts are the inevitable by-products of its processes of rearranging the truth, and it is in the corridors of the Ministry of Truth that Winston meets not only Julia, his love, but also O'Brien, his nemesis, who will tempt him so that all his aberrant tendencies towards independent thinking are revealed and then will break him within the white walls of Room 101.

But there is a section of the Ministry of Truth that is working on the problem of residual doubt. It has come from the opposite direction to Orwell's own conclusion, that there is an organic relationship between language and thought. Freedom of thought and imagination is, in Orwell's writer's view, dependent on a clear, abundant, and supple language; destruction of thought and the elimination of doubt, in the eyes of the theoreticians at the Ministry of Truth, is dependent on the restriction and impoverishment of the language. The result is the strange jargon of clipped and neutral portmanteau words known as "Newspeak" not yet completely achieved when the action of the novel takes place, but well-advanced.

Orwell thought the dangers implicit in his concept of Newspeak so important that he wrote a special appendix to *1984* on "The Principles of Newspeak"; this showed the attention he had paid not only to Communist jargon, but also to manufactured languages like Esperanto, of which his aunt Nellie Limouzin was an exponent, and simplified languages like Basic English, to which he was first favorable and then critical. But the implications of Newspeak are most vividly outlined in the novel itself by a character named Syme who is working on the latest edition of the *Newspeak Dictionary*. Sitting in the cafeteria of the Ministry of Truth, Winston Smith listens to Syme's diatribe, which embodies Orwell's satiric exaggeration of what he believed to be a genuine threat.

> "You think, I dare say, that our chief job is inventing new words. But not a bit of it! We're destroying words—scores of them, hundreds of them, every day. We're cutting the language down to the bone."

After dwelling with almost chop-smacking relish on the joy of destroying words, Syme continues:

> "Don't you see that the whole aim of Newspeak is to narrow the range of thought? In the end we shall make thoughtcrime literally impossible, because there will be no words in which to express it. Every concept that can ever be needed, will be expressed in exactly *one* word, with its meaning rigidly defined and all its subsidiary meanings rubbed out and forgotten....
>
> "The whole climate of thought will be different. In fact there will *be* not thought, as we understand it now. Orthodoxy means not thinking—not needing to think. Orthodoxy is unconsciousness."

So, embedded in the heart of Orwell's most famous and most challenging novel, we find the ultimate issue of politics concentrated in the question of language, which assumes such a central role in the novel that Winston's degradation in Room 101 seems an unnecessary embellishment. Indeed, there is a major thematic division in the novel at this point, for if the desire for power can be satisfied by eliminating thought through a change in linguistic patterns, then human beings become vegetables anyway and there is no need for the Party to think, as O'Brien does, in terms of endlessly repeated cruelty represented in the image of "a boot stamping on a human face—for ever."

In my view the horrors of Room 101 project the quasi-Gothic excesses of a not entirely successful novelist, as Orwell frankly admitted himself to be. The invention of Newspeak reveals Orwell's real journalistic genius and links up with the important aspects of his career, reflecting his pride and reliance as a man-of-letters on language, his awareness as a practicing journalist of the way language had been betrayed in his age, and more remotely but perhaps no less authentically, the sense of awe rising from that Anglican childhood whose memory he so obstinately treasured in his agnostic adulthood: the awe that strikes as one sets out to read the Gospel according to St John: "In the beginning was the Word. . . . " For Orwell, like all good writers, was a word-intoxicated man.

VITA FORTUNATI

"It Makes No Difference": A Utopia of Simulation and Transparency

THE AMBIGUITY OF UTOPIA: UTOPIA AS GAME

Utopian literature is remarkable in being made up of a series of works linked by a tight network of echoes. The paradigm has its own rules and conventions to which all creators of successive utopias refer, to which, indeed, they must refer if they wish to create a utopia. Thus, in order to understand the significance of Orwell's anti-utopia, we must go back to the utopian tradition, for *1984* echoes this tradition. Orwell is mounting a concentric attack not only on the utopian tradition but also on the very structure of a utopia. Orwell's anti-utopia is not a work which lies outside the universe of utopia but both stems from and remains constitutionally within the framework of utopia. In this sense we may see how *1984* marks the end of utopia, or at least, of the possibility of utopia.

We must return first, for a moment, to the archetype of the genre, Thomas More's *Utopia*. Utopia, or the invention of a utopia, is a game based on the possibilities which experience offers, it is an *if* which is explored in all its possibilities. A utopia is not reality, but it is a *possible reality*. The game of utopia, like the game of chess, requires a set of pieces which have to obey certain rules. In order to be complete and well-ordered, the game must impose certain rules on time and space; the *outopos* has its own time and space. In the game of chess, the bishop, knight, rook, and queen simulate a battle; in a utopia, the elsewhere, the journey, the arrangement of a city simulate society.

From *Orwell: Il Testo*, edited by L. Russo. © 1985 by Vita Fortunati. Cento Internazionale Studi di Estetica, Palermo, 1985.

From the very beginning of the genre, utopia has had a ludic quality in that it is a speculative game with reality expressed in terms of a *political proposal* which is set up against reality. *The model suggests a possible reality which could substitute for the existing reality.* A utopia always maintains a close and specific relationship with the sociopolitical environment from which it stems. The alternative proposal which it represents in the form of a radically different society springs from a harsh criticism of the utopian writer's present reality of departure. The essence of utopia is to be found precisely in this shifting of position between a projected environment which is not reality and the actual reality to which the projected environment is in opposition. Utopia is thus a game played between the two poles of reality and fiction. Both the strength and the weakness of utopia rest in the basic underlying ambiguity of the genre. It is a strength in that a utopia represents a tension towards the elsewhere which reveals the ability to *think about the Other,* to go beyond the given facts and reality. It is a weakness because in utopia, in the model, there is the abstraction of the real and its *simplification.*

We have proposed the image of utopia as a game, but we must remember that every match of utopia versus reality reveals different characteristics from those of the preceding bouts since not only is any expression of utopia situated within a complex network of echoes of the preceding utopias, but it also sets up a specific relationship with the present which generates it. Each utopia is characterized by its identity with previous utopias and is distinguished by its diversity from these; thus the tradition of utopia is multiple and multifaceted. The march of utopias is a march of identical elements which are specific in their individual diversity.

Let us turn now to Orwell. In what sense may we speak of *1984* as the end of utopia? Why does Orwell annul the dialectical tension between the two elements which make up the essence of utopia, the tension, that is, between *what is and what should be, between reality and fiction?* In Orwell's work we find the total identification of the model with the reality, there is no longer any difference or distance between them. Everything is utopia, everything is project and fiction, contrast is lost. The projected reality has engulfed and entirely swallowed up reality. Thus utopia is no longer possible because the referent no longer exists and in its place there is the *simulacrum.* The connection with historical reality no longer exists, the possible project exists and is moved by a single energy source, *Power.* It is power which no longer has as its "telos" the organization of society but which is now simply an end in itself, a game played purely for its own sake. History no longer exists, history is a succession of simulacri, a *hyper-*

history. It is a series of games with reality; paradoxically utopia has won because here *utopia finds its final realisation*. An end has been made of the long cavalcade of utopias, the long series of proposals of possible worlds; the projects have been realised. Utopia thus becomes the re-creation of reality, the end of History. In Oceania, history is rewritten, re-created. "All history was a palimpsest, scraped clean and reinscribed exactly as often as was necessary."

The game may now be played *ad infinitum*, the projectualization of possible worlds now has no limits for the real referent has been removed. In Oceania, the Party suppresses all trace of its own historical origins in order to defend the legitimacy of the *perpetual present*, that is, of its own power. "Who controls the past controls the future: who controls the present controls the past."

I shall now attempt to consider the following points in an interpretation of Orwell's novel through a careful analysis of the text: 1) *1984* as the end of utopia; 2) *1984* as utopia as simulation; 3) *1984* as beyond the panoptic utopia; 4) *1984* as utopia as no-difference; 5) *1984* as parody of earlier utopias.

1984 AS THE END OF UTOPIA

At the level of narrative structure, the distinction between reality and fiction, between the world of the reader and the place of the Utopia, has been removed in *1984*. In earlier literary utopias the dislocation was achieved through the journey. The journey emphasized the detachment from the departure reality for the two worlds existed in two different spaces, the utopia was clearly situated in an *elsewhere*, the time and space coordinates of which, however, remained intentionally imprecise. In Orwell's utopia, as in Zamyatin's *We* which stands as the primary twentieth-century anti-utopia model, the journey has been eliminated and the dislocation is now not spatial but temporal.

When Orwell's novel was first published, the title *1984* had the metaphorical function of alluding to a time in the future which was, however, not too distant from the present of the reader. It is interesting to note how the temporal dislocation around which the book is constructed is still effective even today when we have actually reached and indeed passed the year 1984. In my interpretation, this is because the figurative strategies used within the text create an effect of total ambiguity. The ambiguity stems from the difficulty of drawing a clear distinction between dream and reality, between the subjective world and the objective world. The entire third section of the novel is characterized by this blurring of limits. Winston Smith does not know where he is, he cannot tell day from night. He no longer has a sense of time and space. The atmosphere is that of a terrible nightmare dominated by ominous deformed images of animals like frogs and rats and by expressionistic visions of huge women of Swiftian proportions "with great tumbling breasts," of skull-like faces and by repulsive smells of vomit, sweat, reeking breath. Winston Smith lives in a state of lethargy or semiconscious stupor: "He had the impression of swimming up into this room from some quite different world, a sort of underwater world far beneath it." "He moved himself mentally from place to place, and tried to determine by the feeling of his body whether he was perched high in the air or buried deep underground."

Several critics have observed that the opening sentence of the novel, "It was a bright cold day in April, and the clocks were striking thirteen," is a superb example of the technique of defamiliarization [*ostranenie*], the kind of writing that transmits to the reader a shiver of worrying strangeness and unfamiliarity. Oceania is a world half-familiar and half-fantastic, where fantastic is understood in the sense of uncanny. While on the one hand the sentence recalls the conventions of English poetic tradition from Chaucer to Eliot, it nonetheless simultaneously turns these upside down by introducing transgressive elements which do not belong. The phrase "the clocks were striking thirteen" is a violation of the standard code for telling the time in Western society. In Oceania, April is not "wet" as both poetic and folk tradition would have it but "bright and cold." The text abounds with examples like this, examples which bear witness to the elaborate figurative strategy which Orwell uses to distance the reader from empirical facts and push him or her towards a transgressive reading of the rhetoric of the text.

In *1984,* we have lost the clear-cut distinction between the two character-types of literary utopias, the *traveller,* who carries the values of the society of departure, and the *guide,* who is the character within the utopia who expounds the principles on which the utopia world in question is based. Winston Smith, a citizen of Oceania, is ambiguously both inside and outside the utopia.

Orwell's camera moves in close-up or long shot to his characters depending on whether they express the function of the classical dupe of satirical tradition, who is blind to, or incapable of, perceiving the environment around him which he endures passively, or the external eye which can take in and also criticize the dystopic facets of Oceania civilization, thus rendering his relationship with the surrounding world problematical. From this point of view, Orwell brings into the utopia, which generally gives so little attention to individual differences and is utterly devoid of any psychological bent the traditional analysis of characters typical of the novel as literary form. Irving Howe is correct in stating that *1984* must be read as a text in which different genres are interwoven and interact: utopia, romance, satire, essay and standard novel.

The final interview between Winston Smith and O'Brien may be read not only as the rewriting, in terms of parody of the scene of the Grand Inquisitor, but also as the rewriting of the dialogues which typically appear in utopias. This dialogue no longer shows traces of the characteristic dialectical dialogue, expressing a polyphony of voices, but is in reality a simulated dialogue in which the two speakers do not reveal different points of view. Winston is not the carrier of an alternative reality, he is, as we shall see below, the other face of O'Brien, his double. Opposition is not possible in Oceania society. Winston Smith is O'Brien's accomplice in the gratuitous power game because he consciously agrees to take part in it.

1984 AS UTOPIA OF SIMULATION

Oceania is a huge simulacrum of Power, where the sense of the sign no longer connects with a referent. The continually repeated and multiplied images of the enormous face of Big Brother do not connect with anything material, but rather with a vacuum or an absence. Political acts have been reduced to simulated acts, Power has been stripped of its political dimension. The social scene in Oceania is an empty stage on which remain only the signs of a power emptied of all morality and moral principle. It is power which is the object of social demand for signs of power. Thus in Oceania, there are the massive rallies of "Two Minutes Hate" or the public spectacles of the hangings, where methods of mass communication are exploited just as they were in the great Nazi rallies so carefully orchestrated by Albert Speer, the inventor of the terrifying aesthetics of collective gatherings. As political morality no longer exists in Oceania, Power is forced to recreate it by means of the *fiction* of Conspiracy and Scandal. The game of Power is the spectacle which O'Brien has to create for himself, a game which can be infinitely repeated. As O'Brien says to Winston Smith: "This drama that I have played out with you during seven years will be played out over and over again generation after generation, always in subtler forms."

The Power game is a competitive game and in order to play it O'Brien has to train an opponent. It has to be a real opponent, one at his own level, for parity of the contenders is one of the rules of the game. It has to be for the final victory to be full, satisfying and pleasurable. The situation in Oceania is paradoxical, for in order to express itself Power requires resistance and an opponent. The total control which Power holds makes the Power game even more difficult and it is thus the simulation of the opposition which must be as plausible as is possible in terms of simulation. It is for this reason that the novel gives more space to the description of the preliminary preparation than to the ultimate match between O'Brien and Winston Smith.

The relationship between Winston Smith and O'Brien may thus be interpreted as a competitive game for power, a gratuitous game, a game which exists only for its own ends. Here we may again see a clear parody of the utopian ideal in which power is always instrumental.

> The Party seeks power entirely for its own sake. We are not interested in the good of others; we are interested solely in power. Not wealth or luxury or long life or happiness: only power, pure power. What pure power means you will understand presently. We are different from all the oligarchies of the past, in that we know what we are doing. . . . Power is not a means, it is an end.

It is Orwell himself who suggests this interpretation of the relationship between Winston Smith and O'Brien, as the relationship between two players who have accepted the rules of the game, as a framework to the novel by alluding throughout the work to various types of game which we may classify following Caillois' classification as "competition, simulacrum, chance and vertigo." In the final pages of the book, Orwell applies the game metaphor to society as a whole. Winston plays a single game of chess, but it is a game which is entirely simulated and manipulated, because Big Brother has already won, Big Brother always wins.

The game between Winston Smith and O'Brien is characterized by a highly charged emotional content. The two establish between themselves what amounts to a sadomasochistic relationship of victim and torturer. They operate within the same framework for they share and accept the same rules of the game. From this point of view, the figure of Smith, which is generally accepted within Orwell criticism as that of the rebel, in my opinion needs to be rethought and re-analyzed. Winston Smith is far from being merely an innocent victim. He enters the game voluntarily and fully aware; he enters the game knowing that the Brotherhood cannot exist and is only an illusion. "What was happening was only the working-out of a process that had started years ago. . . . He had accepted it. The end was contained in the beginning." The match between Winston Smith and O'Brien can thus be seen as the initiation of Smith to pure power, during which he learns its rules, that is, the rules of the game, by playing it.

1984 MARKS THE TRIUMPH OF THE PANOPTIC SOCIETY WHILE SIMULTANEOUSLY GOING BEYOND IT

In Oceania, the telescreen rules everything and everyone; it becomes the principle of total visual control. The echoes of Bentham's utopia, the *Panopticon,* are inevitable and important.

The Panopticon took form as an architectural project in which the rationalization and the control of space became the exercise and history of Power. The Panopticon is the circular prison with the watchtower at the centre from which the guard can see the prisoners without being seen. Bentham applies the panoptic machine with rigorous thoroughness to all possible real-life uses, prisons, factories, hospitals, mental asylums, schools, wherever a number of people have to be watched over. From this point of view, then, Oceania is the panoptic society *par excellence.* The telescreen is the invisible eye which sees and controls everything. However, while it is true that Oceania represents the panoptic society *par excellence,* it is equally true that it nonetheless marks the end of such a society.

Just as the actual referent of the utopia project has been eliminated, so in the dialectical relationship of Controller–Controlled the telescreen is also a pure simulacrum. Behind the telescreen there is a vacuum and the medium projects the image of a controller who does not actually exist. Bentham's universe presupposed a hierarchical society in which there were well-defined roles and a dialectical relationship between those who watch and those who are watched.

Orwell reduces this tension between the Watcher and the Watched to nothing. In Oceania, everyone is watched, in place of the guard there is the telescreen which is the medium through which the panoptic machine works. In this sense, Orwell goes beyond the panoptic society and presages the endemic widespread presence of television and the hidden power of the media which destroy the distinction between active and passive. During the Two Minutes Hate there is a total, passive enjoyment of the simulation. The image and the model become more real than the real. The telescreen becomes a kind of parody of the religious metaphor of the omnipresent Eye of God which sees you at every moment. From being a metaphor which gave substance to a divine and moral principle, the eye has become a machine for social control.

1984 AS UTOPIA OF NO-DIFFERENCE

In the society which Orwell creates in *1984,* oppositional, binary, Saussurian logic no longer exists. As we have seen, there exists instead the logic of abstract models, uprooted from any actual reference to reality. In the universe of total simulation there governs a total relativity which means manipulation and combination of models. Orwell's Newspeak marks the final death of oppositions and heightens the elimination of dialectic. Now thought is possible only as automatic thought, which does not develop but simply repeats in a stereotypical way the party slogans. Oceania is the world of no-difference, of the interchangeability of terms: war is peace and peace is war. It is a world in which positive and negative generate and replace one another in turn. "It does not matter whether the war is actually happening, and, since no decisive victory is possible, it does not matter whether the war is going well or badly." The phrase which recurs in an almost obsessive manner throughout the novel is "it (the Party) makes no difference," or, in an alternative form, "nothing makes a difference." This above all emphasizes the neutralizing and homogenizing character of Oceania society. The law of equivalence governs everything; it is a world in which dialectic has been eliminated and the sequence of contradiction, alternative and head-on clash is no longer possible. The Party cancels all traces of difference through the elimination of historical memory. Thus history is "vaporized." "And so it was with every class of recorded fact, great or small. Everything faded away into a shadowworld in which, finally, even the date of the year had become uncertain."

The fate of *1984* as a text seems to indicate that the "no-difference" of Oceania society is also the "*in*difference" of our own society, and that there is a close relationship between us as readers and *1984* as text. For it is a text which today, now that Orwell's year has come and gone, seems to run the risk of being safely filed away out of thought, of being defused of its worrying, ominous charge simply because we are afraid of being afraid. It is a text which because of its very popularity, its widespread diffusion, and its notoriety has tempted the fate, and continues to do so, of being tamed and rendered innocuous through familiarity. When we reread Orwell today, we must make the effort to reappropriate the horror which it describes and produces, for this is the very horror which our own society is surreptitiously administering to us daily in small but significant doses.

1984 AS A PARODY OF UTOPIA

In *1984*, Orwell takes the ideas and images with which the utopian imagination had worked in the past and turns them upside down. He makes the language of utopia his own and rewrites it in terms of parody. *1984* sets up an intertextual dialogue with the utopias which precede it and inverts the values of these models using characteristic techniques of parody such as amplification and grotesque.

It is not within the scope of this present study to analyze in detail the many parts of the novel where Orwell may be seen to be rewriting the utopias of the past. However, I shall here concentrate on two or three of the most important *topoi* of utopia literature which Orwell systematically inverts or turns inside out. In this way, the anti-utopia explodes the whole genre of utopia.

The typical utopian city, well-ordered, harmonious and perfect in all its parts, the very layout of which reflects the sociopolitical ideals of the utopian writer, in *1984* is represented by a decaying, bomb-shocked London of ruins and skull-like houses denuded of windows. In the standard utopia there ruled a harmonious relationship between both man and his environment and man and the State. The constant watchful regard of Power in Oceania does not unite its people, but rather isolates and separates them.

As O'Brien says, "It is the exact opposite of the stupid hedonistic Utopias that the old reformers imagined." It is thus in no way a utopia founded on love and justice. "A world of fear and treachery and torment, a world of trampling and being trampled upon. . . . The old civilizations claimed that they were founded on love or justice. Ours is founded upon hatred. In our world there will be no emotions except fear, rage, triumph, and self-abasement."

The total transparency of the standard utopian place which hides nothing of its workings and leaves no shadow of doubt or uncertainty of its motives and functions under the all-pervading light of rationality, honesty and truth becomes in Oceania total invisibility. In Oceania, mirrors do not reflect; glass is opaque. As C. S. Lewis said, a totally transparent world is an invisible world.

The appendix giving details of Newspeak may also be read as a sort of parody of the utopian principle that everything should be apparent at a single glance, including the language. With Newspeak, Orwell ridicules the various different attempts (for example, new alphabets) by earlier creators of utopias to invent a pure, simple language which would be transparent in all its parts. Newspeak is thus a parody of pure and simple language, a language mutilated and homogenized.

Even O'Brien the dictator may be seen as a parody of the creator of utopias, a moralist, censor, pedagogue who wants to reform humanity, as represented by Winston Smith, "the last man" of a generation which is in the process of becoming extinct. O'Brien represents future humanity, the new man, man uprooted from his past culture and history, man with no memory, stripped of his own individual identity and his own past.

As a final point, given the importance with which Orwell invests his anti-utopia, I would like to examine the sections of the novel which deal with torture, the physical suffering of Winston Smith and his relationship with Julia.

These sections are generally seen as a further demonstration of the totalitarianism of Oceania or of any totalitarian utopia and as evidence of the persecution of the individual this entails, coupled with the impossibility of a private life within such a society. This is no doubt true, and Orwell wanted to underline this particular aspect in his work, yet I feel that a more satisfying and complete explanation may be found by considering these areas outside the context of certain aspects of the immediate postwar period and the cultural turmoil of the time in which the book was written.

It seems to me that even in these parts of the novel Orwell is stating his position with respect to the tradition of utopia. As far as the relationship between O'Brien and Winston Smith is concerned, Orwell repeatedly draws into evidence the sadomasochistic component present in the encounter, and in the torture chapter Winston Smith's corporeality is continually emphasized, with no attempt to hide the fact that his suffering is a brutally physical suffering. I would suggest that this is intended as a scorching reminder that points, paradoxically, to the overwhelming absence of such themes in earlier utopias. Utopia, and the whole tradition of utopias, may be seen as a vehicle for political statements. By choosing the literary form of the utopia, writers are able to bring into the open controversial areas of state organization such as the distribution of wealth and class relationships. In this sense, utopia has been a progressive influence, acting as the testing ground for alternative political proposals and the possibilities, both practical and theoretical, of imagining new aspects of the real situation. Orwell, however, has discovered the Achilles' heel of the utopian exercise and in *1984* demonstrates that *Utopia* and its long chain of later imitations may be read as an operation of removal and exorcism of a very different series of difficult, controversial subjects which may be expressed simply as sex and crime.

More's Renaissance rationality, Bacon's proto-Illuminism, Bentham's Utilitarian rationality all reveal an effective phobia for all abnormal or deformed aspects of real life. It is not merely coincidence that the problems of sex, of women, and of crime are not present in any of the earlier utopias. The anthropological model which underlies the utopian tradition is a model of rational perfectibility of both society and man, where reform of the state leads inevitably to the disappearance of all the dark or shadowy aspects of life. This model is shown to be insufficient and structurally unsound in Orwell's *1984*.

Orwell's conviction is that these shadowy aspects are not merely momentary blemishes on the history of mankind and that we must therefore come to terms with sexual tendencies and the physical nature of our bodies. Corporeality is exemplified through physical acts such as defecation and copulation. Swift and Bentham, to name only two of the more lucid creators of utopias, demonstrate a phobia about these aspects of real life which in the utopias of other writers, Fourier, for example, are on the other hand carefully compartmentalized and thus rendered innocuous. In *1984*, the horrendous torture scenes and Winston Smith's physical suffering as well as the debased relationship with Julia serve as a kind of moral blow. Orwell includes them as a sarcastic cry of rage against the systematic removal and ignoring of these aspects in previous utopias.

Finally, and to avoid the risk of being misunderstood, I would say that Orwell is forced to pay a certain price in his attempt to draw attention to and reverse this operation of systematic removal. Orwell has to homogenize the preceding utopias, and thus his reading of them annihilates the different meanings and values expressed in the heterogeneous collection of earlier expressions of the genre. Orwell is forced to place, at least implicitly, Communist, theocratic, right-wing, and left-wing utopias on the same level. Orwell builds up an enemy with his own hands in order to shoot it down, creating the concept of utopia "tout court" without distinguishing one example from another in terms of merit or worth. This method cannot be approved from the point of view of methodology or history. His target thus is utopia understood as a totalitarian phenomenon, which finds its realization in a consolidation of homogeneity, of types, of repetitions, and of orthodoxies. Once he has achieved this transformation, Orwell becomes extremely harsh in his criticism of such a phenomenon, yet it remains a criticism at the highest possible level, as he himself is the first to realize that the terms of the question have changed. The dominant element is now that of the mass society and of its totalitarian mentality: this is finally the society of no-difference, the transparent universe.

The high cost of Orwell's critical transformation of utopia is found in the loss of the highly charged tension of idealism, the missionary zeal and the tang of heresy which works of utopia express. Orwell's own criticism of utopia through *1984* should not be ignored and would seem to me to contradict certain instrumentalizations of his work which have been made and continue to be made.

We must see *1984* therefore as a lucid challenge flung to utopia by an intellectual who always liked to consider himself an "unwanted guerrilla." It is a challenge to utopia as a totalitarian phenomenon in the service of power, a challenge to the utopia which paralyzes the imagination by keeping it under utter control.

Chronology

1903	George Orwell (Eric Arthur Blair) born June 25 at Motihari, Bengal, to a middle-class English family which has been attached to the British colonial administration in India and Burma.
1917–21	After English preparatory schools, scholarship to Eton.
1922–27	Serves with Indian Imperial Police in Burma.
1928–29	In Paris, writes and works as dishwasher.
1930–34	Lives mainly in London. Publishes articles and translations.
1933	*Down and Out in Paris and London.*
1934	*Burmese Days* published in New York, for lack of an English publisher.
1935	*A Clergyman's Daughter.*
1936	*Keep the Aspidistra Flying.* Orwell marries Eileen O'Shaughnessy. Leaves for Spain in December to join anti-Fascists in Barcelona. Serves four months on the Aragon Front.
1937	*The Road to Wigan Pier.* Wounded in the throat, Orwell returns from Spain to England.
1938	*Homage to Catalonia.* After several months in sanatorium for treatment of tuberculosis, Orwell visits Morocco for winter.
1939	*Coming Up for Air.*

1940–43   *Inside the Whale.* Medically unfit for service, Orwell joins Home Guard. Writes and broadcasts for the BBC as wartime propagandist.

1943   Literary editor of the *Labour Weekly Tribune.*

1945   Correspondent for *The Observer.* Orwell's wife dies during surgery. *Animal Farm.*

1946   Rents house on Jura, in the Hebrides.

1947   Intermittent attacks of tuberculosis.

1949   *1984.* Marries Sonia Brownell. Enters sanatorium.

1950   Orwell dies in London, January 21.

1968   *Collected Essays, Journalism and Letters* published.

Contributors

HAROLD BLOOM, Sterling Professor of the Humanities at Yale University, is the author of *The Anxiety of Influence, Poetry and Repression,* and many other volumes of literary criticism. His forthcoming study, *Freud: Transference and Authority,* attempts a full-scale reading of all of Freud's major writings. A MacArthur Prize Fellow, he is general editor of five series of literary criticism published by Chelsea House.

NORTHROP FRYE, Professor Emeritus at the University of Toronto, is one of the major literary critics in the Western tradition. His major works are *Fearful Symmetry, Anatomy of Criticism,* and *The Great Code of Art.*

PHILIP RAHV, Ukrainian-born critic and essayist, was Professor of English at Brandeis University, and cofounded *Partisan Review.* His essays are collected in *Literature and the Sixth Sense.*

MALCOLM MUGGERIDGE, writer and critic, is the author of *The Earnest Atheist: A Study of Samuel Butler* and *The Sun Never Sets: The Story of England in the Nineteen Thirties.*

HERBERT READ was an eminent British essayist and critic. His books include *In Defence of Shelley, Poetry and Anarchism, Reason and Romanticism,* and *English Prose Style.*

LIONEL TRILLING, for many years University Professor at Columbia University, was one of the most eminent critics in American literary history. His works include *The Liberal Imagination: Essays on Literature and Society, Beyond Culture: Essays on Literature and Learning,* and *Sincerity and Authenticity.*

PHILIP RIEFF, Benjamin Franklin Professor of Sociology at the University of Pennsylvania, is the author of *Triumph of the Therapeutic: Uses of Faith after Freud* and *Freud: The Mind of the Moralist.*

153

RICHARD WOLLHEIM teaches philosophy at the University of London and at Columbia University. His books include *On Art and the Mind* and *Sigmund Freud*.

NICHOLAS GUILD is a novelist. His books include *The Berlin Warning, The Linz Tattoo*, and *The President's Man*.

JEFFREY MEYERS is Professor of English at the University of Colorado, and is the author of *A Reader's Guide to George Orwell* and *D. H. Lawrence and Tradition*.

CLEO McNELLY KEARNS teaches English at Rutgers University. She is the author of a forthcoming study of T. S. Eliot.

ROY HARRIS is Professor of General Linguistics at Oxford. His books include *The Language Myth* and *Approaches to Language*.

GEORGE WOODCOCK teaches at the University of British Columbia. His books include *The Crystal Spirit: A Study of George Orwell, Anarchism*, and studies of Pierre-Joseph Proudhon and Thomas Merton.

VITA FORTUNATI is Associate Professor of Modern Foreign Languages at the University of Bologna. Her books include studies of the dandy in English literature and of literary utopias.

Bibliography

Atkins, John. *George Orwell: A Literary Study.* London: John Calder, 1954.

Bloom, Harold, ed. *Modern Critical Interpretations: George Orwell's 1984.* New Haven, Conn.: Chelsea House, 1987.

Brander, Laurence. *George Orwell.* Toronto: Longman, 1954.

Burgess, Anthony. *1985.* London: Hutchinson, 1978.

College Literature 11, no. 1 (Winter 1984). Special George Orwell issue.

Eagleton, Terry. "George Orwell and the Lower Middle-Class Novel." In *Exiles and Emigrés: Studies in Modern Literature.* New York: Schocken, 1970.

Freedman, Carl. "Writing, Ideology, and Politics: Orwell's 'Politics and the English Language' and English Composition." *College English* 43, no. 4 (April 1981): 327–40.

Glicksburg, Charles I. "George Orwell and the Morality of Politics." In *The Literature of Commitment.* Lewisburg: Bucknell University Press, 1976.

Greenblatt, Steven, J. *Three Modern Satirists: Waugh, Orwell, and Huxley.* New Haven: Yale University Press, 1965.

Gross, Miriam, ed. *The World of George Orwell.* New York: Simon & Schuster, 1972.

Harris, Harold J. "Orwell's Essays and 1984." *Twentieth Century Literature* 5, no. 4 (January 1959): 154–61.

Hollis, Christopher. *A Study of George Orwell: The Man and His Works.* Chicago: Regnery, 1958.

Howe, Irving. "Orwell: History as Nightmare." *American Scholar* 25 (Spring 1956): 193–207.

———. *Orwell's 1984: Text, Sources, Criticism.* New York: Harcourt, Brace & World, 1963.

———. *1984 Revisited.* New York: Harper & Row, 1983.

Jensen, Ejner J., ed. *The Future of 1984.* Ann Arbor: University of Michigan Press, 1984.

Justman, Stewart. "Orwell's Plain Style." *University of Toronto Quarterly* 53, no. 2 (Winter 1983-84): 195–203.

Kalechofsky, Roberta. *George Orwell.* New York: Frederick Ungar, 1973.

Knapp, John V. "Orwell's Fiction: Funny but Not Vulgar." *Modern Fiction Studies* 27, no. 2 (Summer 1981): 294–301.

Kubal, David L. "Freud, Orwell, and the Bourgeois Interior." *Yale Review* 67, no. 3 (March 1978): 389–403.

――――. *Outside the Whale*. Notre Dame, Ind.: University of Notre Dame Press, 1972.

Kuppig, C. J., ed. *1984 to 1984*. New York: Carroll & Graf, 1984.

Lewis, Robin J. "Orwell's *Burmese Days* and Forster's *Passage to India*: Two Novels of Human Relations in the British Empire." *Massachussetts Studies in English* 4, no. 3 (1974): 1–36.

Lief, Ruth Ann. *Homage to Oceania: The Prophetic Vision of George Orwell*. Columbus: Ohio State University Press, 1969.

Macdonald, Dwight. "Varieties of Political Experience." *The New Yorker* (March 28, 1959): 132–47.

McNamara, James, and Dennis J. O'Keeffe. "Waiting for 1984." *Encounter* 59, no. 6 (December 1982): 43–48.

Modern Fiction Studies 21, no. 1 (Spring 1975). Special George Orwell issue.

Norris, Christopher. *Inside the Myth: Orwell: Views from the Left*. London: Lawrence & Wishart, 1984.

Patai, Daphne. *The Orwell Mystique: A Study in Male Ideology*. Amherst: The University of Massachusetts Press, 1984.

Poznar, Walter. "Orwell's George Bowling: How to Be." *Wascana Review* 14, no. 2 (Fall 1979): 80–90.

Rees, Sir Richard. *George Orwell: Fugitive from the Camp of Victory*. London: Secker & Warburg, 1961.

Roazen, Paul. "Orwell, Freud, and *1984*." *Virginia Quarterly Review* 54 (1978): 675–95.

Sandison, Alan. *The Last Man in Europe: An Essay on George Orwell*. London: Macmillan, 1974.

Slater, Ian. *The Road to Airstrip One*. New York: Norton, 1985.

Small, Christopher. *The Road to Miniluv: George Orwell, The State, and God*. London: Victor Gollancz, 1975.

Stansky, Peter, and William Abrahams. *The Unknown Orwell*. New York: Knopf, 1972.

Trilling, Lionel. "Orwell on the Future." *The New Yorker* (June 18, 1949): 78–83.

Van Dellen, Robert J. "George Orwell's *Coming Up For Air*: The Politics of Powerlessness." *Modern Fiction Studies* 21, no. 1 (Spring 1975): 57–68.

Vorhees, Richard J. "*1984*: No Failure of Nerve." *College English* 18 (November 1956): 101–02.

――――. *The Paradox of George Orwell*. Lafayette, Ind.: Purdue University Studies, 1961.

Walter, Nicolas. "George Orwell: An Accident in Society." *Anarchy* 8 (October 1961): 246–55.

Watt, Alan. "George Orwell and Yevgeny Zamyatin." *Quadrant* 28, nos. 7–8 (July–August 1984): 110–11.

Williams, Raymond. *George Orwell*. New York: Viking, 1971.

――――, ed. *George Orwell: A Collection of Critical Essays*. Englewood Cliffs, N.J.: Prentice-Hall, 1974.

Wilson, Angus. "Orwell and the Intellectuals." *The Observer* (January 24, 1954): 8.

Wilson, Edmund. "George Orwell's Cricketing Burglar." *The New Yorker* (May 25, 1946): 86–90.

Woodcock, George. *The Crystal Spirit: A Study of George Orwell*. Boston: Little, Brown, 1966.

———. "Utopias in the Negative." *The Sewanee Review* 64 (1956): 81–97.

World Review, n. s. 16 (June 1950). Special George Orwell issue.

Zwerdling, Alex. *Orwell and the Left*. New Haven: Yale University Press, 1974.

Acknowledgments

"Orwell and Marxism" by Northrop Frye from *Northrop Frye: On Culture and Literature: A Collection of Review Essays* edited by Robert D. Denham, © 1978 by the University of Chicago. Reprinted by permission of the University of Chicago Press. This essay originally appeared in *The Canadian Forum* 26 (December 1946).

"The Unfuture of Utopia" by Philip Rahv from *Literature and the Sixth Sense* by Philip Rahv, © 1969 by Philip Rahv. Reprinted by permission of Houghton Mifflin Company and the author. This essay originally appeared in *Partisan Review* 16, no. 7 (1949).

"Burmese Days" by Malcolm Muggeridge from *World Review* n.s. 16 (June 1950), © 1950 by *World Review*. Reprinted by permission of the Australian Institute of International Affairs (Queensland Branch).

"1984" by Herbert Read from *World Review* n.s. 15 (June 1950), © 1950 by *World Review*. Reprinted by permission of the Australian Institute of International Affairs (Queensland Branch).

"George Orwell and the Politics of Truth" by Lionel Trilling from *Commentary* 13, no. 3 (March 1952), © 1952 by the American Jewish Committee. Reprinted by permission of the estate of the author and Harcourt, Brace, Jovanovich.

"George Orwell and the Post-Liberal Imagination" by Philip Rieff from *The Kenyon Review* 16, no. 1 (Winter 1954), © 1954, 1986 by Philip Rieff. Reprinted by permission of the author and *The Kenyon Review*.

"Orwell Reconsidered" by Richard Wolheim from *Partisan Review* 27, no. 1 (Winter 1960), © 1960 by Partisan Review, Inc. Reprinted by permission of the author and *Partisan Review*.

"In Dubious Battle: George Orwell and the Victory of the Money God" by Nicholas Guild from *Modern Fiction Studies* 21, no. 1 (Spring 1975), © 1975 by the Purdue Research Foundation. Reprinted by permission of the Purdue Research Foundation, West Lafayette, Indiana.

"Orwell's Apocalypse: Coming Up for Air" by Jeffrey Meyers from *Modern Fic-*

tion Studies 21, no. 1 (Spring 1975), © 1975 by the Purdue Research Foundation. Reprinted by permission of the Purdue Research Foundation, West Lafayette, Indiana.

"On Not Teaching Orwell" by Cleo McNelly Kearns from *College English* 38, no. 6 (February 1977), © 1977 by the National Council of Teachers of English. Reprinted by permission of the National Council of Teachers of English.

"The Misunderstanding of Newspeak" by Roy Harris from *Times Literary Supplement* (January 6, 1984), © 1984 by *TLS*. Reprinted by permission.

"George Orwell and the Living Word" by George Woodcock from *Queen's Quarterly* 91, no. 3 (Autumn 1984), © 1984 by George Woodcock. Reprinted by permission of the author.

Index